Jan —

There's no time like NOW.

Enjoy!

Praise for *Business at the Speed of Now*

"Bernard recognizes the magic of being able to say yes to the customer. He describes how existing systems and processes stand in the way of yes, and lays out what it will take to unleash your people and organization so they can give your customers what they want, when they want it."

—Leo Hopf
author of *Rethink, Reinvent, Reposition*

"John Bernard, with masterful precision and grace, defines what we know is happening in business today but may have trouble defining. Through strokes of his pen, he clearly articulates what needs to be considered and weighed and defines clear steps to the future, while honoring the past and embracing the Now with full force. Bravo John for capturing the essence of what needs to happen in business Now!"

—Nicole Lipkin
PsyD, MBA, author of *Y in the Workplace:*
Managing the "Me First" Generation

"John Bernard has a magical ability to inspire, motivate, and lead organizations. He is the rare mentor we all seek, whether one-on-one or in front of a thousand people. He shows you how to see the gold nuggets in the muddy water of your business and gain astonishing productivity from the most average employee."

—Mark Cleveland
Serial Entrepreneur

"John McKay, the great coach of the USC Trojans, once responded to a question about his team's execution: 'I'm all in favor of it.' He should have spent some time with John Bernard and learned how to manage the Now. John (Bernard, that is) has fixing things in his blood. He may have been only five years old when Coach McKay uttered those words, but I have no doubt that John Bernard could have turned that whole season around. John is a teacher, but first he is a student. He has an uncanny knack for figuring stuff out, flipping it upside down, and making it work better, faster, and most importantly, producing results. I know. I hired him as a consultant many years ago at Nike.

This book is a must read for anyone who has a management job to do. Just do it."

—Bob Harold
Chief Financial Officer (former), Nike

"To me there is nothing more critical than engaging our 120 talented dentists in creating an extraordinary, patient-focused practice. By implementing the NOW Management System we have achieved across-the-board results beyond anything we had imagined."

—**Dr. John Snyder**
CEO, Permanente Dental Associates,
Kaiser Permanente Health Plan

"The customer satisfaction challenges we faced were costing us a lot and we couldn't figure out how to resolve them on our own. Mass Ingenuity brought us a clear, logical, and effective approach, so that we could quickly make improvements and sustain them. Our investment in Mass Ingenuity has proven to be an outstanding decision."

—**Ellen Steele**
VP, Customer Service, The Standard

"Early in the process of implementing the management system, you could see the silos of the organization melting away. A clear focus on our purpose developed and we were able to move forward in ways not possible before."

—**Scott L. Harra**
Director, Department of Consumer and
Business Services, State of Oregon

"Mass Ingenuity is a company that is easy to brag about. Wow, what a positive change it made in our company and the people who worked there. After owning a business for more than 25 years, with Mass Ingenuity we were supercharged and invigorated with the excitement of a new business! Our relationship with Mass Ingenuity not only catapulted our company into the future with innovative new thinking and great results, it brought many employees great personal growth. A wonderful by-product of the system was a tool that visually proved to our prospective and current clients that we were the right supplier for them. The results were priceless!"

—**Marti Lundy**
CEO and Cofounder (retired), Moore Electronics

"To stem the tide of lost market share, we needed an external perspective to help us look closely at our whole process for scheduling appointments. Mass Ingenuity brought us the skills and perspective we needed to hit our goal. We moved our time-to-first-appointment from 6.7 weeks to 2.8 weeks, and we have sustained the improvement. This opened the door for program growth, one that had been closed for 10 years because of this chronic problem."

—**Ray Chesley**
Director, Strategic Initiatives,
Dental Operations, Kaiser Permanente

"I have known John Bernard for over 15 years, having worked with him on continuous improvement strategies at Columbia Forest Products. *Business at the Speed of Now* is John's crescendo regarding survival in the coming economy. I thoroughly endorse this new work; John is a master of hurdling the theoretical and making things practical and deployable."

—Brad Thompson
President and CEO, Columbia Forest Products

"John is a gifted presenter. He speaks with clarity and passion about change and transformation. He articulates the frustration many have been feeling about work and the work environment but are unable to put into words. John's enthusiasm for change and passion for success is infectious. His message is inspiring and energizing."

—Fariborz Pakseresht
Deputy Director, Oregon Youth Authority

"Mass Ingenuity's management system has had a dramatic positive impact on my organization. The implementation of the rollout was very well organized, engaging our leadership team to embrace and leverage the planning tools well beyond my initial expectations. Though still early in the deployment of the system, we are more focused, better informed, and fact-based in our decisions. I am pleased with our progress to date and have great ambitions for widespread deployment throughout our global operations."

—Harve Bellos
President and CEO, Paccess Global

"This is a book every CEO who's paying attention to the forces that most threaten his or her business must read. Every CEO wants his or her organization to be managed in the Now. I have known John for many years, and the respect he has among high-technology executives is well deserved, because of his pragmatic, common-sense perspective and counsel on how to build great companies."

—John Harker
Chairman and CEO (former),
InFocus Systems

"This is the book that we have been looking forward to—simple and to the point. It takes complex management theories and practices and presents them as common sense, so you can make them common practice in your organization."

—Ted Barber
Director, Operations,
The Coca-Cola Company

"*Business at the Speed of Now* is grounded using sound feedback and measurement principles. John offers a road map on how to deploy these time-tested axioms in today's fast-paced and rapidly changing world. He provides managers with ideas and techniques that resonate with today's techno-savvy workforce. This is not a one-size-fits-all book, but a flexible approach aligned to your strategy. This is your strategy implementation manual."

—Lawrence P. Carr
PhD, Professor, Babson College

"Running a large, complex company and aligning every employee to what you are trying to get done is hard but essential work. John's book hits right at the heart of the challenge every CEO faces, getting everyone focused and executing effectively on what matters most."

—Rick Wills
Chairman and CEO (former), Tektronix

"The speed of business today is incredible, and those unable to stay ahead of information overload and analysis paralysis are dead. John is shedding light on a new system of management that allows all employees to act 'in the moment' with clarity and common purpose. This is a powerful concept that will redefine our understanding of management and success."

—Ralph Quinsey
President and CEO, TriQuint Semiconductor

"John has reached into his deep well of transformational experience to build a management system that helps any organization simultaneously address the fundamentals of running its business while working breakthrough concepts to take it to the next level. At the same time, it aligns the organization from top to bottom, so that you can realize the full potential of Lean and Six Sigma through an engaged workforce. He peppers his talks with rich stories that any of us can relate to, bringing his system alive in ways that only a bruised and scarred practitioner can."

—David Almond
Director, Office of Transformation, Department of
Administrative Services, State of Oregon

business
at the
speed
of
now

business

FIRE UP YOUR PEOPLE,

at the

THRILL YOUR CUSTOMERS,

speed

AND CRUSH

of

YOUR COMPETITORS

now

JOHN M. BERNARD

WILEY

John Wiley & Sons, Inc.

Published by John Wiley & Sons, Inc., Hoboken, New Jersey.

Published simultaneously in Canada.

For general information on our other products and services or for technical support, please contact our Customer Care Department within the United States at (800) 762–2974, outside the United States at (317) 572–3993 or fax (317) 572–4002.

Wiley publishes in a variety of print and electronic formats and by print-on-demand. Some material included with standard print versions of this book may not be included in e-books or in print-on-demand. If this book refers to media such as a CD or DVD that is not included in the version you purchased, you may download this material at http://booksupport.wiley.com. For more information about Wiley products, visit www.wiley.com.

Library of Congress Cataloging-in-Publication Data:

Bernard, John M., 1955-
  Business at the speed of now: fire up your people, thrill your customers, and crush your competitors / John M. Bernard.
    p. cm.
  Includes index.
  ISBN 978-1-118-05401-7 (cloth); ISBN 978-1-118-17535-4 (ebk);
  ISBN 978-1-118-17536-1 (ebk); ISBN 978-1-118-17537-8 (ebk)
  1. Management—Technological innovations. 2. Employee motivation. 3. Success in business. I. Title.
  HD30.2.B468 2012
  658—dc23

                                                              2011029129

Printed in the United States of America

10 9 8 7 6 5 4 3 2

To my wife, partner, and primary cheerleader, Lannah.
Thank you for your endless encouragement and tireless patience.

Contents

Appendix 215

The NOW Speedometer:
Doing Business at the Speed of Now 215

Acknowledgments

When this journey began I did not realize that it takes a village to write a book. I owe a great debt of gratitude to all the villagers who made it possible.

No one individual helped more than Michael Snell, my literary agent and writing collaborator. He demanded my best effort and often cracked a big whip to get it. I will never forget his frank appraisal of my initial query and manuscript (long ago shredded): "You have managed to obscure some very interesting ideas here." That comment marked the first of many challenging milestones on the road to publication.

Another great ally on the journey, marketing and branding expert Betty Rauch, helped me clear the fog surrounding the positioning and messaging of my ideas. I am so grateful for her enthusiasm for this project and her candid, unflinching feedback.

I offer special thanks to Patricia Snell, who read and reread every chapter with a keen eye toward stronger storytelling and a tighter presentation.

My heartfelt appreciation also goes out to my teammates at John Wiley, in particular my editor Shannon Vargo and her capable assistant Elana Schulman, not to mention Lauren Freestone and Janice Borzendowski. Their advice, edits, and advocacy for *Business at the Speed of Now* have proven invaluable.

My business partners picked up a lot of slack while I was writing the book. In particular, Aaron Howard steered the ship at Mass Ingenuity, while Ed Israel, Kelly Ferguson, Jean Baumann, Jim Clark, Tom Moore, and Kelly Jensen gave me their unflagging support. Christine Barker, Will Sandman, and Mary Snyder lent me their eyes and ears along the way, and Shannon Bodie wrangled all the art for the book. Thank you all!

I must also acknowledge the help and support of our strategic partners and friends, especially Dr. Michael Rowney, Kendall Kunz, L. B. Day, Dr. Robert Harmon, Beverly Stein, Sandra Suran, Fred King,

Barry Wilber, and Barb Gaffney. Larry Briggs of V2A Leadership deserves special recognition.

Finally, I feel blessed to have learned so much over the years from wonderful clients: Dr. John Snyder, Marti Lundy, David Almond, Sarah Gates, Colette Peters, Fariborz Pakseresht, Dick Pedersen, Joni Hammond, Kris Kautz, Scott Harra, Michael Jordan, Matt Hixson, Brad Thompson, Bob Dunn, Bob Harold, Rich Walje, Jason Landmark, Bruce Kerr, Rod Cruickshank, Eric Parsons, Scott Eave, Mark Cleveland, Christophe Sevrain, Denise Jones, and Mike Green.

Every writer needs a muse, and I feel fortunate to have found mine in Teresa Roche, chief learning officer of Agilent Technologies. I am also lucky to count Bill Walker, Wally Pfeiffer, Robin Anderson, Robert Franz, Jack Warne, Jay Wilt, Frank Wagner, and Jennifer Bosze among my dear friends, colleagues, and supporters.

My five-year-old twins, Christian and Jacqueline, put up with an absentee father for a few long months, while my grown daughters Ryann, Erin, and Ashley offered their wisdom, their Millennial generation stories and their "Go, Dad, Go!" support and understanding throughout the process.

Surrounded by such strong allies, friends, supporters, and believers, I kept on working, even on those days when I felt like the village idiot.

Introduction

Outreach and building community with readers is the single most important thing you can do for your book these days," said Random House editor Anne Groell in Laura Miller's April 11, 2011 article in *The New Yorker* about author George R. R. Martin. Over the years, Martin, author of *A Game of Thrones*, the first in his multivolume fantasy series *A Song of Ice and Fire,* has followed his editor's advice. Using Facebook, Twitter, and an active website, Martin won the hearts of millions of fans and sold a whopping 15 million books worldwide.

While Martin employed social media tools to build a vast audience for his work, he also found that they can wield a double-edged sword. When he failed to deliver a much-anticipated fifth volume in the series, he suffered painful cuts from that sword. Martin's once-loyal fans, angered by repeated delays in the publication of the next book, launched a scathing cyberspace assault on him. The disaffected readers saw themselves as customers, not just fans, and they believed that gave them the right to complain about poor service. Martin's online community manager, Ty Franck, referred to the angry readers as the "entitlement generation." "[Martin] thinks they're all younger people, teens and twenties. And that their generation just wants what they want, and they want it now. If you don't get it to them, they're pissed off."

Having become an author myself, I got to thinking about Martin's predicament. I believe that the readers of this book are my customers. Whether you run a Fortune 500 company or a brand-new start-up, whether you manage a force of a thousand or merely one other person, and regardless of the type of job or the level at which you work in your organization, you feel a need to learn more about what's going on in this brave new world of business. You may belong to the entitlement or millennial generation, or you may count yourself part of generation X or a member of the baby boomer club. In any case, your business has needs, and they need attention now. I invite you to tell me exactly what you think of this book. Please join the *Business at the Speed of Now* community at: www.business-at-the-speed-of-now.com.

I wrote this book because businesses must learn how to function more effectively during what is the biggest economic shift in more than a century. The world is moving rapidly from a global economy driven by mass production to one driven by mass customization. The mass production revolution (that was *then*) made it possible for businesses to deliver the same product to millions of customers. The mass customization revolution (this is *now*) demands we vary our products and services to meet the unique needs of customers who want what they want now. To do that, business leaders and managers must fire up their people and enable them to seize opportunities and solve problems almost instantly. In the battle for these impatient customers, you must act more quickly than ever before or run the risk of losing out to more nimble competitors. In short, you must do *business at the speed of now*.

In this new world, three game-changing drivers make it possible for any organization to grow prosperously: social media, cloud computing, and the "millennial mind-set." Social media quickly creates vast powerful communities by connecting people inside and outside an organization; cloud computing, defined on Wikipedia simply as, "Internet-based computing, whereby shared resources, software, and information are provided to computers and other devices on demand, as with the electricity grid," provides a cost-effective means for giving workers the resources they need to solve problems the instant they arise; and the millennial mind-set demands that it all happens in the now.

A mass customization economy demands mass ingenuity, mass engagement, and mass action. You must give your people on the front lines the ability, the skills, and the tools to say yes to customers who not only want the next new product or service now, but who also demand unprecedented quality, affordable prices, exceptional service, ethical behavior, environmental and social responsibility, and a handsome payoff on their investments. All at the same time.

During my career as a worker, manager, executive, and business owner, I have built and tested a management system designed for the era of mass customization. In this book I distill the principles and practices that forward-thinking leaders and managers can use to make their own organizations move faster and, at the same time, be more productive and more profitable. I have applied what I have learned to almost every conceivable type of organization, from a one-man start-up business financed on a shoestring to a multibillion-dollar financial services company where I oversaw nearly 1,000 people and an $80 million budget. In addition to running businesses, I have worked with such companies as Nike, Kaiser Permanente, PacifiCorp, Baxter Healthcare, and Agilent Technologies. With my team at Mass Ingenuity, I have also applied these ideas with great results in private sector businesses, nonprofits, and governmental agencies, including many in the State of Oregon.

To bring to life the principles and practices of doing *business at the speed of now*, in the pages ahead I include more than 60 stories of success and failure. In many cases, the name and nature of a business have been disguised in order to honor the need for confidentiality, or, in some cases, to protect the guilty. In each of these examples, at first mention, I enclose "The Company Name" and "The Manager Name" in quotes rather than give actual names; but rest assured, all of these stories are true.

Each chapter in the book concludes with the NOW Speedometer, a device you can use to measure your organization's current capability to do *business at the speed of now*. The speedometer will help you assess the dimensions of speed addressed in that chapter.

The map in Figure I.1 provides an eagle's-eye view of the journey ahead.

Chapter 1, "Thriving in the Now: Prepare for Yes," explores the revolutionary forces that make "YESability" the ultimate value proposition. This first chapter reveals exactly why organizations must shift from a *then* to a *now* management system.

In Chapter 2, "Making the Shift to Now: Put an End to Then," you will learn about the "Seven Deadly Sins" of management and how they squander the talent and resources desperately needed to succeed in a now economy. This chapter offers proven ways to counter those sins by creating total employee engagement.

Chapter 3, "Seizing the NOW Opportunity: Drive Growth with Yes," describes the NOW Management System and shows you how to use such a system to mobilize your people to meet internal and external customer needs in the now. The Three Gears of the NOW

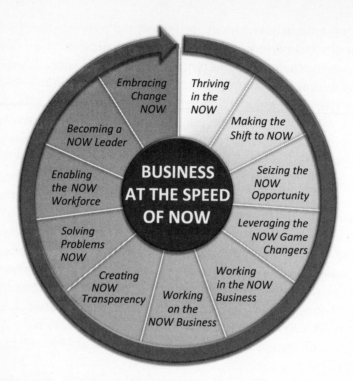

FIGURE I.1   Business at the Speed of Now

Management System focus on eliminating fear in your workforce, reducing variation in everything you do, and overcoming the constraints in your business that inhibit progress toward your goals.

Chapter 4, "Leveraging the NOW Game Changers: Gain the Speed You Need," examines the three major forces—social media, cloud computing, and the millennial mind-set—that offer managers powerful tools for accelerating the transition from then to now.

In Chapter 5, "Working in the NOW Business: Create the Context for Speed," you will see how you can develop the right context for your employees, connecting them to and aligning them with the goals of the business. The chapter emphasizes the importance of viewing management as a system that functions for one and only one purpose: to fulfill the mantra of now: Every Opportunity, Every Employee, Every Time.

Chapter 6, "Working on the NOW Business: Achieve Critical Breakthroughs," tackles the all-important subject of achieving breakthroughs. It provides tools for getting everyone involved in planning and executing initiatives, and it connects such popular techniques as Lean, Six Sigma, and process improvement to the need for now action.

The millennial mind-set demands transparency. Leaders pay a lot of lip service to the concept, but Chapter 7, "Creating NOW Transparency: Close the Execution Gap," shows you exactly how to install it in your organization with formal business reviews.

Chapter 8, "Solving Problems Now: Equip Everyone with the Core Skill," introduces a powerful Seven-Step Problem-Solving methodology. It follows one company as it wrestles with a puzzling setback. Your people can use this methodology to solve all the big and little problems that pop up every day in their routine work.

Nothing blocks the transition from *then* to *now* more than fear. Chapter 9, "Enabling the NOW Workforce: Banish Fear, Build Trust," details the ways in which you can conquer fear by striking the right balance between order and freedom. In this chapter you'll learn how to move your people through the Seven Stages of YESability, a key element in the transition from *then* to *now*.

The transition will never take place without a new style of leadership. Chapter 10, "Becoming a NOW Leader: Stop Bossing, Start Teaching," stresses the need to stop bossing people around and to start teaching them. By asking questions rather than providing answers, you demonstrate your own shift from telling people how to solve problems to guiding them to search for their own solutions.

Finally, Chapter 11, "Embracing Change Now: Accelerate the Shift," draws from the latest neuroscience research to give you practical tools for inspiring people to embrace and accelerate organizational change, without which all efforts to do *business at the speed of now* would ultimately fail.

In the Conclusion you will find a compact summary of the steps outlined in the book, including a specific plan for continuing to move your organization from *then* to *now*.

Enough preamble. As the poet E. E. Cummings so aptly put it, "There's a hell of a good universe next door; let's go."

Thriving in the Now

Prepare for Yes

Katy, two years out of engineering school and a new recruit at software developer "Expedite," has just arrived at her Silicon Valley cube for a one-week stint on the graveyard shift as a technical support specialist. She has volunteered for this assignment because she's eager to see what happens on the front lines with customers she would otherwise never meet.

Grabbing her Red Bull, she logs in to Expedite's new management system designed to satisfy customers at the speed of their need.

Katy barely settles in when her Skype rings. Onto the screen pops the clearly irate face of the chief information officer of TexTech, the huge account in Ireland that Expedite won just last week.

"Six of our production facilities are down," bellows the CIO, "because your damned software crashed! We need this fixed, and we need it fixed now!" Katy's heart races. She knows that her actions during the next few minutes will determine whether the CIO decides to stick with the new software or dump it.

"I'll get back to you in 10 minutes," Katy promises.

Immediately she sends an internal distress tweet to the software team in Vietnam. In less than a minute she's on Skype as the engineers in Saigon access relevant documents and data from the cloud. Their real-time conversation includes "tag" searching of blogs, video references, and critical documents. The inference engine suggests the

```
┌─────────────────────────────┐
│            DREAM            │
│      Every Opportunity      │
│       Every Employee        │
│         Every Time          │
└─────────────────────────────┘
```

FIGURE 1.1   Dream

"best-fit" materials to review. The engineers quickly spot the problem, a recently discovered bug that the application maintenance department in Paris had fixed and validated hours earlier; they immediately make the necessary change in their cloud application.

When Katy Skypes the CIO, not only has he calmed down, he's thrilled with the swift response. "I didn't think you guys could solve the problem this fast. You're amazing!"

As Katy finishes the call with the customer, she picks up her Red Bull. "Still cold," she marvels. Her smartphone chimes with a text from her boss.

"Checking in. Everything Okay?"

"All good here," she texts back.

In a traditionally managed organization, Katy would have needed to turn the customer problem over to management, and that would have delayed the solution by hours, if not days. Fortunately, however, Katy works for a company that does *business at the speed of now.*

By design, conventional management systems prevent both speed and customization at a time when employees and customers alike clamor for both. If your business doesn't provide it, your competitors will.

Customers increasingly demand a yes answer to each and every question they ask. They want what they want, and they want it now. This turns the world of management on its head. Managers simply cannot keep using a system that creaks along, getting bogged down in protocol or bureaucracy. Companies must evolve or die. Once the need for speed burst into the business environment, it changed the game. Today, competitive success demands a new approach to management, one that enables employees at all levels to solve problems and seize opportunities autonomously and instantaneously.

Our Love of Speed

An advertisement for the Pony Express printed in a California newspaper in 1860 read: "Wanted. Young, skinny, wiry fellows. Not over 18. Must be expert riders. Willing to risk death daily. Orphans preferred."

The forerunner of Federal Express ran weekly. Instead of overnight, communications took 10 days at 10 miles per hour to get from St. Joseph, Missouri, to Sacramento, California. A half-ounce letter cost $425 in today's dollars. Riders received $100 a month in a time when unskilled laborers earned a mere $4.

Amazingly, the famed Pony Express lasted only 18 months. By 1861, the first telegraph poles began dotting the countryside. And within the decade the tracks of the first transcontinental railroad ran from sea to shining sea. What propelled these developments? A love of speed and, more specifically, a passion to get vital information more swiftly.

Over the past hundred years, farsighted entrepreneurs have invented planes, jets, the fax machine, and, in the past two decades, the internet and mobile electronic devices to support the need for speed. Now anything anyone needs to know can travel at the speed of light, circling the globe 7.4 times in 1 second or traveling to the moon and back in 2.6 seconds (see Table 1.1).

TABLE 1.1 History of Speed

Mode	Speed/mph	Downsides	When
Stagecoach	5	Dangerous and unreliable	1766
Pony Express	10	Expensive and dangerous	1860–1861
Telegraph	4,900,000	Unreliable, few locations	First in 1861, last in 2006
Railroad	5–50	Expensive, few locations	1869 first transcontinental
Airplane	80–600	Expensive to operate	First 1848, common by 1940s
Jet	768	Expensive	First in 1930s, common by 1960
Fax	4,900,000	Specialized equipment	First 1924, popular 1970s
E-mail	669,000,000	Requires computer	First 1965, popular by 1990
Texting	669,000,000	Limited information	First in 1992, popular by 2000

mph = miles per hour

Since nothing moves faster than the speed of light, information will never flow any faster, although bandwidth expansion allows greater and greater quantities of information and richer and richer media ("Yes, there are plenty of apps for that!") to come speeding down the information highway. Having achieved near-instant access to the information they want and need, both customers and employees now expect speed every second of every day.

The ability to receive information with a single click of the mouse or a tap on the screen sets expectations high for getting anything you want. If you can access the cast and storyline of the latest Academy Award–winning film on your smartphone or iPad, then why can't you get your cable provider to solve a connectivity problem in seconds? Why can't you get that new LCD 55-inch television installed this afternoon? People want all sorts of stuff, and, more and more, they want it now.

Twitter's language of hash tags and short URLs can be used as a window through which millions of people can peer to see what's going on now, whether in the world of celebrities and global corporations or in the lives of friends or colleagues. A follower can access breaking news from CNN, the musings of business icon Jack Welch, details of the latest costumes worn by Lady Gaga, the most recent developments in the NFL or NBA, and the latest news from the Ford Motor Company, not to mention updates from the president of the United States or even the author of this book. (Follow me on Twitter: @johnmbernard.)

What does all this mean to today's business leaders and managers? Quite simply, it means that you must find ways to do business at the speed of everyone's need. You must find better ways to fire up your people, thrill your customers, and race past your competitors— now. This book will explore the principles and practices that leaders and managers can use to thrive in a world where change happens so fast you can only see today in your rearview mirror.

The Power of Yes

"Hello, I'm having trouble with my HD DVR," Harley told the DirecTV service representative, who immediately said, "Thank you for being such a long-time customer." For over 15 years Harley had remained loyal to the satellite television provider that he had championed to all his friends and neighbors on Cape Cod, many of whom also became enthusiastic customers. Whenever he had called with a problem, a DirecTV technician had always solved the problem immediately or quickly escalated it up to someone who could. But not this time.

The technician said, "I see we've run through the troubleshooting protocols. You probably need a new unit, but you'll need to talk with technical support."

"Can't you just authorize a new HD DVR and save me and your company a lot of time?" Harley had grown impatient with trying the same fixes over and over, all to no avail.

"No sir, this is the way we have to do it."

A half hour later Harley had talked to three different people, told the same story to each, ran the same diagnostic tests of the system, and still had not received authorization for a replacement device, even though he was a long-time customer and paid extra each month for a total equipment protection plan.

Finally, the third technician offered to connect Harley to someone in senior management. A senior manager reviewed the case, asked the same wearisome questions, and, finally, authorized the replacement machine.

Harley then asked the woman a simple question: "Why don't you allow your front-line people to make an obvious decision and save me and yourselves a lot of hassle and money? If this happens to me again, you'll turn me into a former customer."

"Well, sir," responded the manager, half jokingly, "Management needs *something* to do."

Subsequently, when one of his tennis buddies asked him about switching from cable to satellite TV service, Harley did not recommend the move.

While reasonable customers don't mind answering a few reasonable questions, no one likes being treated like an idiot or a crook, or being taken on an agonizing journey through the messy decision-making maze of an organization where management "needs something to do." Customers simply don't care about a company's internal procedures and policies; they want a speedy answer to a specific question, and the answer they want to hear is yes!

A company's failure to solve the customer's problem now can mean the beginning of the end of a relationship, as it did for Harley. It can also mean the beginning of a new relationship with a competitor. As happened in the DirecTV example, a long-time loyal customer lost confidence in a firm with which he had enjoyed a 15-year relationship, not over a string of bad experiences but over company procedures and policies that had prevented it from saying yes and saying it now. It happens every day as businesses lose customers for reasons they never even see. In reverse, a surprise accommodation can turn a prospective buyer into a loyal customer.

Yes derives its power from the fact that it saves customers time; and time, like low tide, waits for no one. No one can ever buy more of it; it continually slips away, and when it's gone, it's gone forever. When a customer hears a prompt yes, she can happily move on to something else she needs to do. When she hears no, especially after waiting for over an hour to hear it, she feels as if she's been robbed of something irreplaceable.

Customers also value yes because it respects their needs and makes them feel good, whether they are dealing with an insurance provider or the Department of Motor Vehicles. Can you think of a better definition for customer service than "making the customer feel good?" That feeling lies at the heart of every customer relationship, and yet companies forget that fact all the time when they take loyalty for granted.

My wife and I felt our loyalty taken for granted recently when our long-time insurance company, a name-brand outfit (always top-rated by *Consumer Reports*) failed to say yes. We had always liked the service this company provided, but after an industrial van smashed into my rear bumper while I was stopped at a signal waiting for the left-turn light to turn green, I ran into a snarl of red tape.

Even though my insurer ended up not paying a dime on the claim (the company that owned the vehicle that hit me did), while dealing with the incident, my insurer discovered I had not updated them on the fact that I had recently begun using my personal vehicle for business purposes. Both my wife and I held interminable conversations with a service rep, who implied that we were purposely trying to deceive a firm that also carried our home, auto, umbrella, and life policies. We paid this company a lot of money, only to listen as its representative made us feel like crooks.

The relationship soured instantly. Why, you might wonder, didn't I express my unhappiness to upper management? The hassle had already cost me more time than it was worth, so instead I began looking for an insurer that would give me the respect a valuable customer deserves.

Yes helps maintain beneficial relationships; no gives customers the impression that they are not valued or that the company does not value the relationship.

I Want My Yes Now!

My literary agent and collaborator, Michael Snell, recently installed two new computers in his office, a PC purchased from Dell and a Mac ordered from Apple. When I asked him which system he liked best, he sighed. "Oh, both systems work fine for our purposes, but let me tell you, customer service is night and day. When the PC crashed due to a virus, I spent three hours on the phone with service reps at Dell's facility in Mumbai, first with a computer voice (you know, 'if X press Y, if A press B'), then to someone who routed me to the hardware department, when I really needed help with the software; and finally to 'Rick' who was extremely polite but painfully slow. The fix ultimately took two hours and cost me $59."

Michael then experienced a problem with his Mac's capability to communicate with his office printer. "I called Apple Care," he explained, "and within three minutes I was talking to a technician who recorded my iMac's serial number, then patiently but swiftly walked me through a rather complicated series of steps that involved eliminating a tiny piece of corrupted code in the operating system. That did the trick. The whole affair took 15 minutes and did not cost me a dime."

Both Dell and Apple have access to the same technologies to manage their customer interactions, so why the difference in the customer's experience? One of the companies implements yes now, the other limps along with maybe someday. Technology has enabled a revolution, but you must join it, not sit on the sidelines, because customers *expect* yes now.

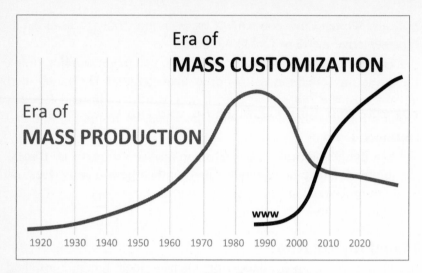

FIGURE 1.2 Mass Production versus Mass Customization

Businesses can say yes now because a whole host of new technologies and applications have finally made it possible to do so. Companies now operate in a new Era of Mass Customization, where customers enjoy nearly unlimited options to satisfy their needs and appetites. Mass customization, a term Stan Davis popularized in his 1987 book *Future Perfect*, aptly describes the internet's impact on the marketplace. No longer must they put up with the "one size fits all" approach of the old Era of Mass Production (see Figure 1.2).

In Chapter 2, I closely examine the impact of mass customization on management, but for now just keep in mind this basic definition for the term: The use of computer-aided systems to produce custom output.

Why does that matter? Computer-aided systems change the value-creation game because they combine the low unit cost of mass production with the flexibility of individual customization. While mass production supplied large volumes of identical products produced at a low cost, mass customization offers individually differentiated products manufactured at or near mass production costs. Mass production once drove the global economy, and still plays a major role in emerging economies, but mass customization increasingly defines a new economy, where companies can say yes to customers and give them what they want when they want it. Of course, businesses have always striven to do that, but now they *can* do it. Three factors are facilitating the transition from mass production to mass customization.

Social Media, Cloud Computing, and the Millennial Mind-Set

Although technological tools are constantly evolving, social media, cloud computing, and the millennial mind-set will continue to advance the progress of this transition because each helps companies satisfy the consumer's appetite for yes.

Social media keeps people connected to information and to each other. Social media, from Facebook, Twitter, and LinkedIn to YouTube, Foursquare, and Groupon, enable users to share their thoughts, activities, accomplishments, and their likes and dislikes, the instant they occur.

Customers can instantly offer feedback or issue complaints. Companies can instantly obtain feedback from customers, or tell them about new products, special offers, and useful tips about using their products. Of course, that free flow of transparent feedback can sometimes prove embarrassing.

Witness the battle between United Airlines and a musician named Dave Carroll. When the airline's baggage handlers badly damaged his $3,500 Taylor guitar on a flight from Halifax, Nova Scotia, to Omaha, Nebraska, United's customer service personnel refused to take responsibility for the mishap or compensate Carroll for his loss, claiming he had failed to make a claim within the company's stipulated "standard 24-hour timeframe." Carroll said later, "I alerted three employees, who showed complete indifference toward me." In response, he wrote a song about the incident ("I should have flown with someone else, or gone by car, 'cause United breaks guitars"), which he posted on YouTube. Within a day 150,000 people had viewed it, and within a year it had garnered a whopping 9 million hits. The *London Times* estimated that, in the end, the 18-month-long public relations fiasco cost United Airlines $180 million dollars in lost revenue, plus the expense of rebuilding its reputation.

Interestingly, Taylor Guitar responded to Dave's video with a post on YouTube to help guitar lovers everywhere, explaining that most airline employees don't know that people are permitted to carry guitars on board, as long as they keep them in their cases, and offering to help any guitar player who may be in need of a repair.

Some companies discover the power of social media the hard way. Aaron Howard, president of Mass Ingenuity and a loyal customer of the car sharing and car club enterprise, Zipcar, suffered a series of bad experiences over a two-day period. While returning a car one evening, Aaron found that not only had someone taken his designated parking space, he could not find any other space to park the car. Zipcar customer service offered no help whatsoever. Thirty minutes later, Aaron finally found a spot to park the car. On his next interaction with Zipcar, he went to the designated space to fetch the vehicle he had reserved, only to discover that another customer had not yet returned that car. Zipcar could offer no nearby alternative. Aaron might have overlooked these inconveniences had Zipcar not announced a big rate increase mere days after a customer service rep had convinced Aaron to "upgrade" to a new program with a 10 percent discount. The higher rate more than obliterated the supposed savings.

Aaron tweeted his dissatisfaction to his followers, including Zipcar. Within minutes 30,000 people and Zipcar itself knew all about Aaron's frustrations. A Zipcar supervisor who had been monitoring Twitter called Aaron within 10 minutes to assure him that the company would redress his grievances. Although, initially, the customer service representatives did not respond properly, social media ended up forcing the company to resolve Aaron's issues. He immediately tweeted his followers to tell them that Zipcar had done the right thing.

The second force, cloud computing, changes the game because it dramatically drives down the cost of computing. Basically, cloud computing involves moving from applications run on a specific computer's hard drive to those run on the internet, or, metaphorically, "in the cloud." When Sherry Swachhamer, the chief information officer of Oregon's Multnomah County, switched her agency from Microsoft's desktop Outlook to Google Apps, a cloud alternative, she achieved an estimated $500,000 reduction in annual costs for the 4,500-employee organization.

In a 2009 white paper titled "The Benefits of Cloud Computing," IBM estimated that cost savings from such a switch would start at

20 percent. A study released the same year by the Silicon Valley–based research and consulting firm The FactPoint Group cited cases where the cloud helped organizations reduce the time it takes to convert to new technology by as much as 80 percent. Still in its infancy, cloud computing represents a solution to the ever-increasing acceleration of costs for traditional approaches to information management. Perhaps more importantly, when you transport data to the cloud, you make it easily accessible to employees who need it in order to act swiftly and avoid customer relations catastrophes like the one United Airlines suffered when it stonewalled Dave Carroll's complaint.

The third, and perhaps most transformative force has resulted from the coming of age of the now generation, the millennials. This generation of consumers and workers has grown up living in the now. Unlike preceding generations, they have never waited for much of anything. Their mind-set, which combines skill in social media and all the latest communication devices with an appetite for instant gratification, has profoundly influenced the workplace and the marketplace. As more and more businesses embrace the "need for speed" aspects of the millennial mind-set, management must change not only the way it operates but also the way it thinks about doing business. Whether you serve as the managing partner of a regional accounting firm, work as the lead software developer in a booming iPhone app company, or manage one small bank, your colleagues and your customers expect you to manage your enterprise in a way that says yes now.

An executive at SupplyWorld, a global supply chain company, explained that he hadn't given much thought to how the millennials and social media were influencing change until he became a grandfather. "My daughter and her husband wanted us to be the first to know that she was pregnant with our first grandchild, so they dropped by the house Saturday afternoon. We were thrilled, of course, but even more delighted when we could share it with the whole family, who arrived at our house after Shannon tweeted everyone that we were celebrating."

When the executive went to his office on Monday morning, the incident clearly in his mind, he peppered the company's chief information officer with questions about how SupplyWorld could take advantage of social media in the marketplace. "What would happen,"

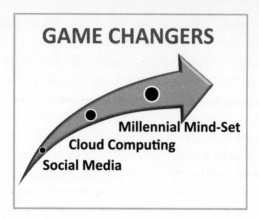

FIGURE 1.3   NOW Game-Changing Drivers

he wondered, "if we flashed a message out to all of our customers about a big one-time freight discount? How many do you think would 'join the party' and place early orders?"

In Chapter 4, we will more fully explore these three NOW drivers (illustrated in Figure 1.3) and how to leverage them.

Mass-Customize Me, Please!

Suppose you need a logo for your new restaurant, "Sparklefish," which specializes in fresh seafood at affordable prices. You don't know any local graphics artists but learn from a friend that she used 99designs.com to get that lovely logo for her bakery. "Just go to their website," she advises. "You'll be amazed how easy it is to get help from great designers around the world." You like that idea because you cannot afford to waste a lot of time on the project. You're busy supervising installation of the restaurant's new appliances and lighting fixtures and don't have the time to interview various design firms or wait for bids on the project.

Seventy-two hours later, you've invested a scant 20 minutes and $360 on the 99designs.com service and have narrowed your choices down from 144 designs to 2 options that beautifully capture Sparklefish's brand and mission. You select an aqua-colored salmon dancing with a bright red lobster.

Sites like 99designs.com allow a business access to a large pool of experts, quickly and affordably, enabling the business to come away with a unique solution tailored to its needs. Rather than one anonymous customer contacting one equally anonymous supplier, Sparklefish's business owner formed a relationship with 144 providers. Then she picked the designer who best understood and related to her needs. She got her yes, and she got it now.

For a century, consumers have enjoyed the fruits of mass production and welcomed the fact that their new Model T Ford, Motorola television set, or Hoover vacuum cleaner were identical to the ones owned by friends and neighbors. While that market reality still applies to many consumer items, a growing number of options are available for an increasing number of products and services.

The Great Recession of 2008, sparked by careless mortgage financing practices and greedy Wall Street dealings, presented businesses with both a problem and an opportunity. Yes, the economy sputtered and drove the unemployment rate through the roof, but it also forced business leaders to rethink the way they do business, developing leaner operations while at the same time vastly increasing customized solutions for their customers. It forced them to grapple with the facts that globalization enables choice, choice increases the necessity to customize, and competitive pressure drives down prices. Five years from now you may look back and see the recession as a milestone on the path from mass production to mass customization.

The constant development of new technologies, and the changes they bring to the business world, render obsolete the stiff old bureaucratic management systems that dictated business workflows and decision making for over a century. Even before the recession, companies were looking for new ways to do more with less. Social media, cloud computing, and the millennial mind-set aid them in that quest.

Buyers expect more from sellers in terms of product features and reliability, the speed with which new products come to market, the swiftness of after-purchase service, and the agility with which sellers jump on the next big thing.

In November 2010, mere months after Apple introduced the iPad, Samsung launched the Galaxy Tab, with features not available on the iPad: a camera (two, in fact), the capability to run Web videos written in Adobe's Flash software, and multitasking. Apple not only reacted to Samsung's challenge, the two companies since then probably have raced through three more competitive cycles. Until recently, salespeople at Best Buy only needed to keep abreast of one new model per year from each television manufacturer every year. Now they must get up to speed on new models from such manufacturers as Samsung every four months.

This customization does not come without cost. It can take a significant investment and resources to fashion an organization that can deliver products and services; and it takes time and money to adopt a management system that enables an organization's people to make now a daily reality. Technology greatly streamlines the automation of custom responses, and a proven approach such as Lean simplifies the processes that deliver customization. Lean, which traces its origins to Toyota's Just-in-Time Production System, helps companies do more with less. While it began as a manufacturing philosophy, companies today apply it to every function, including management, in their effort to eliminate waste.

The agility and efficiency a company needs to flourish in a world of mass customization depends on establishing new systems and embedding them deeply in the organization. It's not just the people who meet and greet the public, sell them stuff, or provide after-purchase service and care who must operate in the now. Everyone from the board of directors to the fellow who polishes the lobby floors at night must embrace the now mentality and utilize the tools that enable them to improve everything they do. Like any engine, every part plays an essential role. If you want to know which parts might stall your own organization, look for the weakest ones. Wherever you find constraints that inhibit making decisions and doing business, that's where the system will either slow up or shut down. The new marketplace realities demand the sort of highly agile, waste-free, and cost-effective management system you'll encounter in the pages ahead.

Enabling Your Organization's YESability

Betty Rauch, a marketing and branding consultant in Manhattan, tells a story about a 175-year-old company that has adopted technologies that enable it to move swiftly, respond quickly, and offer solutions at all levels of the organization. When Betty needed to give a token of appreciation to the retiring executive director of a nonprofit organization, she ordered a small crystal apple from Tiffany & Company, America's oldest and most prestigious jeweler. She wanted the company to etch the gift with a simple "Thank You." When Tiffany delivered the little apple to her apartment, she opened the blue box with anticipation, only to find that the apple bore no inscription. Her heart sank. The nonprofit was planning to present the retirement gift at a Saturday dinner, and there Betty sat at 10:30 on Thursday evening with little time to remedy the situation. "Oh, well," she thought. "They say that their phones are open til 11:00. Might as well let them know they let me down."

To her surprise, when she dialed the number for Tiffany's customer care department, she found herself talking to a real live person, rather than the computer voice she had expected. When she heard "Good evening, this is Tiffany's, how may I help you?" she thought she actually heard a smile in that cheerful voice. After Betty explained her problem, the customer care rep promised to look into it immediately and call back within a half hour. "Yeah, yeah," thought Betty. "Like that's going to happen."

Surprisingly, 15 minutes later, the Tiffany's rep called Betty with the good news.

"We'll have it delivered to your home no later than Saturday morning with the etching you ordered. And, to make up for the inconvenience we have caused a valued customer, please keep the other apple as a gift from Tiffany & Company. You see, Ms. Rauch, you are the apple of our eye!"

What did Tiffany's customer service representative accomplish? She found a way to say yes now. And in the end she not only satisfied an unhappy customer, she created a loyal champion, who will encourage everyone she knows to shop at Tiffany (see Figure 1.4).

YESability depends on many factors, such as front-line responsibility for solving problems, and the communication and system tools needed to solve them; but it begins with management understanding those factors and ensuring that the people who first encounter customer problems possess the tools, skills, information, and authority they need to say yes now. Management must also make sure that all the behind-the-scenes workers who never see a customer (the

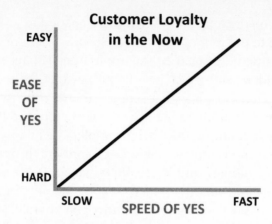

FIGURE 1.4　Customer Loyalty in the Now

engraver at Tiffany, for example) understand their role in delivering solutions at the speed of now.

In the now, managers do not, as one writer once wryly observed, "herd cats," by which he meant vigilantly overseeing and correcting the effort and progress of all the people under their command to ensure that everyone keeps scurrying in the right direction. Rather, in the Era of Mass Customization, they must implement and rely on a management system that enables each and every one of their people, whether they ever see a customer or not, to make quick, smart, and productive decisions.

For an organization to function in the now, its managers must provide every employee with five crucial elements:

1. Context ("Where are we going?")
2. Accountability ("What role do I play?")
3. Skills ("What abilities must I possess?")
4. Facts ("What data must I access to make decisions?")
5. Authority ("Do I enjoy the freedom to act without fear of reprisal?")

To enable YESability, managers must have put these crucial elements in place before the moment of truth arrives in the form of a first-time order or an angry call from an irate customer. The bottom line? Management's work today should center on enabling immediate

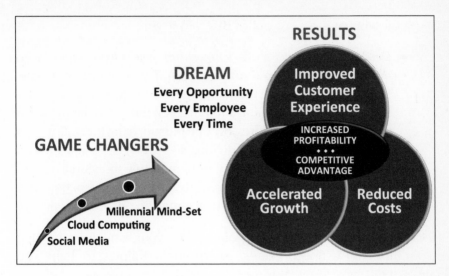

FIGURE 1.5 NOW Drivers to Results

action and ensuring that all action aligns with the direction and goals of the business. It requires an about-face just as revolutionary as the one managers made at the dawn of the Era of Mass Production.

What makes a Tiffany & Company or an Apple Computer or any other great company tick? Their people quickly seize every opportunity that comes along, no matter how trivial. All those seized opportunities, from the smallest to the biggest, accumulate over time to improve customer experience, reduce costs, accelerate growth, and ensure increased profitability and competitive advantage (see Figure 1.5).

The NOW Speedometer

Throughout the chapters of this book you will find many opportunities to analyze and score your organization's performance across a variety of different competencies, and at the end of each chapter you will find a measuring tool that determines an organization's NOW speed. Your score will indicate the degree to which your organization manages in the *then* or manages in the *now*. As you complete each chapter's NOW Speedometer you can accumulate the scores in the Appendix.

You will get the most out of this tool if you:

◆ *Decide whether to score your team, your department, your division, or the overall organization.* Do only one at a time. Trying to do them all at the same time will cause you to lose focus on the level of the organization that concerns you the most. An entrepreneur might score only one person, herself, while a team leader will score many individuals. A CEO, of course, would score the entire organization, not any single individual.

◆ *Avoid overthinking your answers.* Rely on your gut reaction. Too much thinking can cause you to get hung up on too many details.

Pause a few minutes at this point and try your hand at completing your first NOW Speedometer. An example follows to help you understand how to use this tool.

Example

Here's how one hypothetical manager completed the tool. "Kathy Stiles" runs the plant at "Clean-and-Press" (CP), a large dry cleaning establishment, where she oversees the work of six people. With a passion for delighting every CP customer, Stiles takes a hard look at her team. Her thinking goes something like this:

Item One: Which statement better describes her operation: "We say no to special customer needs," or "We try hard to say yes to special customer needs"? Well, they're not very flexible. Stiles recalls losing a customer recently because the woman did not want CP to iron the collars on her blouses, preferring to do them herself. Stiles's plant couldn't handle that request. Stiles scores her department a –1 in the NOW Speedometer's "THEN –1" column.

Item Two: Stiles asks herself which statement best describes CP: "We *immediately* say no to special customer requests," or "We *immediately* say yes to special customer requests"? Stiles remembers another situation when a local restaurant wanted assurance that CP did not use certain chemicals that irritated the sensitive skin of one of its waitresses. It took a week to get an answer back to the customer. On the other hand, Stiles almost always responds to customer requests and complaints the same day via e-mail. She records a 0 in the middle column and goes on to complete the Speedometer.

Stiles then completed the Speedometer using this same thinking process (see Table 1.2).

TABLE 1.2 NOW Speedometer Example

Then	−1	0	+1	Now
We say no to special customer needs	−1			We try hard to say yes to special customer needs
We immediately say no to special customer requests		0		We immediately say yes to special customer requests
We only authorize our people to say no	−1			We enable our people to say yes
We treat every customer the same way	−1			We treat every customer as a unique individual
We ban the use of social media at work			+1	We encourage the use of social media at work
We have not developed a cloud computing strategy		0		We have developed a strategy for moving as much as possible to the cloud
We believe that millennials don't understand what it takes to succeed in the real world			+1	We welcome the millennial mind-set
Subtotals	−3		2	
Working in the Now **NET SCORE**		−1		

TABLE **1.3** NOW Speedometer 1: Working in the Now

Then	−1	0	+1	Now
We say no to special customer needs				We try hard to say yes to special customer needs
We immediately say no to special customer requests				We immediately say yes to special customer requests
We only authorize our people to say no				We enable our people to say yes
We treat every customer the same way				We treat every customer as a unique individual
We ban the use of social media at work				We encourage the use of social media at work
We have not developed a cloud computing strategy				We have developed a strategy for moving as much as possible to the cloud
We believe that millennials don't understand what it takes to succeed in the real world				We welcome the millennial mind-set
Subtotals				
Working in the Now **NET SCORE**				

Add this score to the consolidated scorecard in the Appendix.

■ ■ ■

Complete the Speedometer for Working in the Now (Table 1.3) and add your net score to the summary sheet in the Appendix.

Your net score indicates the degree to which your organization either functions in the then or manages in the now. As shown in Figure 1.6, scores can range from −7 to +7. A score of −7 indicates that your organization functions entirely with a mass production mind-set, whereas a score of +7 suggests it effectively manages in the now.

2

Making the Shift to Now

Put an End to Then

On a pitch-black night, a nuclear submarine slashes full speed through the icy waters of the Irish Sea. The captain orders his radio operator to repeat his warning to the vessel lying directly in their path a few miles ahead.

"Again, this is the *USS Montana* requesting that you immediately divert your course 15 degrees to the north to avoid collision, over."

An immediate response crackles through the sub's speakers. "Please change *your* course 15 degrees to the south to avoid collision." The captain stares at the blinking green dot on the *Montana's* radar screen.

He grabs the microphone and bellows, "This is Captain Hancock, and you *will* divert your course, over!"

Again, the response comes instantly. "Negative, Captain, I'm not moving anything. Change your course, over." The calmly unyielding voice further infuriates the captain.

"I am commander of the *USS Montana*, the second-largest vessel in the North Atlantic fleet," roars the captain. "You *will* change your course 15 degrees north, or I will be forced to take measures to ensure the safety of this ship, over!"

After a tense pause, the calm voice responds, "This is a lighthouse, mate. It's your call."

While apocryphal, this story illustrates how a leader can stubbornly operate under invalid, even dangerous, assumptions that defy common sense. Like the sub's captain, leaders who cling to erroneous assumptions put their entire organization at risk.

While you might expect traditional management approaches to change course in the wake of the transition from mass production to mass customization, too many leaders keep plowing ahead on the same old course, oblivious to the impending crash and the threat to their people's welfare and survival.

You cannot expect to sail safely through the choppy waters of today's tumultuous business environment if you do not give your people the freedom and tools they need to seize each opportunity and solve problems quickly and efficiently. This includes everyone in the organization, from the front line to the executive suite.

Shifting from Then to Now

Imagine recently appointed CEO "Kathy Taylor" receiving a report that shows her software company (an illustrative firm I'll refer to as "BearPaw" throughout the book) has for the third straight quarter failed to hit delivery targets for its best-selling software product. Kathy, uncharacteristically, raises her voice during a meeting with her senior staff. "This has got to stop! No matter how often I explain the importance of accountability, we keep missing our shipping dates."

Kathy's loud voice catches everyone by surprise, especially "Bill Anders," the founder and former CEO, and now chairman, who, 18 months earlier, had tapped Kathy for the CEO position. She won the job because she had built a solid reputation as an executive who always delivered results. Now she was floundering. That made her feel frustrated, disappointed. "I'm at a loss, Bill. What am I missing?" she asks. After all, she had always turned in such stellar performances as a project leader. "I am doing *everything* I did in the past, but it just isn't working."

Bill shakes his head. "Maybe we need to change course and try something new."

Like many CEOs who can't see what they don't see, Kathy was unaware of what *wasn't* happening at BearPaw. Back at her old company, Kathy was unaware of the invisible now-oriented management system that had made it so easy for her to hit one home run after another. BearPaw has not built a NOW system. And just as Kathy couldn't see the NOW system at her old company, she can't see the THEN thinking that lies beneath the surface at BearPaw. In both cases, she didn't see the underlying mental models, assumptions, behaviors, and tools that drive the success or failure of an organization. Like the submarine captain, Kathy didn't always know what she didn't know.

Kathy and many other managers find it difficult to replace the outdated model because they don't even recognize the underlying assumptions that guide their own actions. Everyone has grown up working within the framework of some model and may never have questioned its underlying logic, purpose, or values. People naturally do what they've seen others do. Like Kathy, who worked for an effective manager and emulated what he did, they win a promotion and then repeat what they did before their advancement, hoping it will lead to yet another step up the corporate ladder. When the old ways no longer get results, they feel blindsided.

To succeed in the new Era of Mass Customization, managers must learn to do things differently.

As shown in Table 2.1, mass production (*then*) relies heavily on centralized control and specialization, whereas mass customization (*now*) relies heavily on decentralized autonomous action. This shift completely changes everything you do to make your business succeed: how you motivate and reward your people; how your people interact with customers; how speedily your company acts and reacts in the marketplace; how you design the architecture of your organization; how people acquire, assimilate, distribute, and use data and information; how every employee makes decisions; and how you ensure continual improvement.

Given the often-invisible nature of management assumptions, you must bring them up to the conscious level before you attempt the shift from *then* to *now*. Remaining stuck in the THEN loop will inevitably lead to problems (see Figure 2.1). Your people will grow dispirited, your customers will defect, and your competitors will overtake you. Clinging to the outdated model, you may desperately seek new solutions that you hope will improve results, adopting and prematurely rolling out such tried-and-true tools as Lean, Six Sigma,

TABLE **2.1**   Mass Production versus Mass Customization

	Mass Production	Mass Customization
Output	High Volume, No Variety, Low Cost	High Volume, Customized, Low Cost
Customer Strategy	Standardized Offering	Customization to Need
Required Agility	Slow	Fast
Driver	Managerial Hierarchy	Customer Need
Organizational Logic	Functional	Process Centric
Decision-Making Authority	Centralized	Distributed
Knowledge Strategy	Specialization	Generalization
Knowledge Use	Management	All Levels
Use of Data	Reports, Analysis	Decision Making
Improvement Strategy	Big Ideas	Incremental
Problem Solving	Ad Hoc, Intuitive	Standard Methodology, Fact-Based

and the Balanced Scorecard, only to find that they also fail to deliver desired results.

In sharp contrast, the NOW loop creates clarity and focus to guide and inspire quick action at all levels of the organization, as illustrated in Figure 2.2. With the context clear, many modern management tools

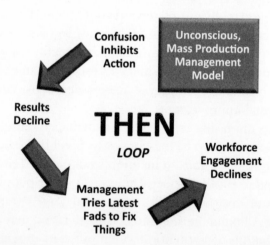

FIGURE **2.1**   THEN Loop

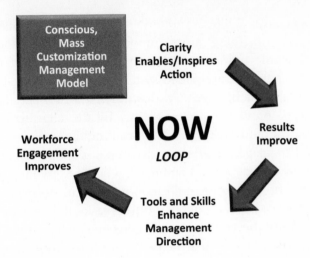

FIGURE 2.2 NOW Loop

can add value. The new way of thinking about your business will pay off handsomely as everything and everyone in the organization works together to fulfill a common vision.

That Was Then, This Is Now

I remember witnessing my dad fire one of his workers. He did it the way he had seen his own father do it at the family-run auto repair business. The boss and his employee would get swept up in a series of escalating arguments. The employee would finally lose his temper and take a swing at the boss. The boss, quickly ducking, would shout, "You're fired!"

No matter what the task, people learn through observation. In fact, most people prefer to learn by watching a skilled person do the job. Of course, that form of learning works well only if the other person possesses excellent skills.

People augment their observations with training, reading, and, in some lucky cases, with coaching or mentoring from someone who knows the ropes. Their ideas about management come via the same routes and settle into the unconscious mind.

Managers, making the shift from *then* to *now* thinking, can take comfort in this: Ever since Henry Ford invented the Model T over 100 years ago, the old thinking has been practically built into their management DNA. While the automobile changed the world forever, Ford created something more important than the Model T. He invented a whole new way of doing business, one that relied on a highly efficient and disciplined system of management. His "mass production" approach drove costs down. This transformed the "horseless carriage," previously enjoyed only by the elite, to a product within grasp of the burgeoning American middle class.

At Ford, managers made the decisions; workers followed their orders. The system depended on breaking down everything into small tasks, which the company could train workers to do over and over again. The faster workers could perform the tasks, the more they would lower the cost of the end product. Management became preoccupied with time-motion studies that helped them turn work into a highly repetitive process—what some critics called a brain-dead process—essentially eliminating all independent thinking on the assembly line.

Ford and other proponents of the new system defined the functional disciplines of modern organizations: engineering, accounting, sales, marketing, manufacturing, and even management. A unique language and toolset emerged for each of these disciplines, which colleges and universities eventually added to their business curricula. Thus, each new discipline became its own self-contained silo of expertise.

The system delivered spectacular results. U.S. productivity turned the country into a global power. Mass production created greater wealth for more people than any other system of management in the history of the world.

Ford's concept remains the model of modern management, embedded deep in most managers' unconscious minds. Every day they rely on his concepts without even pausing to think. Therein lay the seeds of today's problems.

In the business world today, most businesses have not moved sufficiently, if at all, from mass production to mass customization logic. Regardless of the type of business you manage, your customers are demanding more and more customization. Yet, your mass production thinking may be humming along in the background and preventing you from making the shift.

Mass production logic insists that you slow down the inputs in order to speed up the outputs. Since it requires cast-iron consistency, mass production cannot easily cope with a lot of creative thinking because new ideas, especially imperfect ones, disrupt the machine's efficiency. That explains the old logic's preference for centralization, functional silos, and the careful management of all ideas. Resist new ideas, it argues, because the ones that end up not working will create a mountain of rework that can slow an already plodding system down to a crawl. Only those at the top of the food chain, the experts, can decide which ideas merit introduction into the system. On a practical level, this causes bottlenecks, because the experts cannot possibly evaluate even a fraction of the new ideas that come along.

In today's business world you must not turn your back on new ideas, even the little ones, even ones that seem a little crazy, because they may propel you ahead of your competitors. You need new ideas, and you need them now. In the world of mass customization, agile competitors who seize and exploit the best new ideas will clobber leaders who cling to the old logic. In our speed-driven world, the new logic insists that every worker make important decisions and take decisive action now (see Figure 2.3).

In a mass production world, front-line managers listen to the engineers and their bosses; they then communicate their directives to the workers. They do not get paid to listen to and implement employee ideas. Interestingly, in the early days of mass production, management revealed its view of the role workers played in the system, referring to them disparagingly, as "wrenches" or "hammers" or "hands" or "oilers" or "grease monkeys"—mere extensions of the machines they operated.

In the *then* world, management never worried about employees understanding the why behind their bosses' directives. Input from the workers did not matter. Neither did it matter if workers could make no sense of the direction their bosses gave them. Today, workers need to take autonomous action, and to take that action they need to understand much more about the company, its direction, and the part management expects them to play in achieving its mission.

FIGURE 2.3 Clarity Leads to Action

The Seven Deadly Sins of Management

Some years ago I attended a meeting where I found myself seated at the head table with, among others, the keynote speaker for a big local chapter event of the American Electronics Association (now TechAmerica), David Galvin, then chairman and CEO of Motorola. Motorola, at the top of its game, had just won the first-ever Malcolm Baldrige Award, the national quality award instituted by the U.S. Congress.

I posed an innocent question to Galvin's associate, Motorola's vice president of quality, seated at my left. "So Motorola knows how many times the phone rings in customer service before it gets answered? And, am I correct to say it knows the yield, cost, and cycle time of its production and its engineering processes?" The executive nodded.

I continued my questioning: "How do you know your management process is working? What do you measure to know that your system of management is effectively running the company?"

That question prompted a look of puzzlement.

That moment marked an epiphany for me. It suggested that not even the executives at the best-run company in the United States were thinking about management as a process. When many executives talk about management, they talk mostly about small-m "management," or boss-to-subordinate management (managing people). Somehow they didn't see big-M "Management" as the mother of all business processes. Much of process improvement focuses on the reduction of variation because variation causes waste, and waste can add enormous costs to running a business. Yet most managers, especially those who have worked for several companies during their careers, will quickly agree that few business processes display *more* variation than the management process. And the chief indicator of management variation is confusion. The Seven Deadly Sins of Management contribute to that confusion.

The Seven Deadly Sins of Management

1. *Lack of Clear Direction:* If people don't know the organization's destination, they can't spot opportunities to help it get there.

2. *No Line of Sight:* If people can't see how their work connects to the destination, they won't make the best possible decisions in their daily work.

3. *Unclear Accountability:* If people don't know what others count on them to do, they won't do it.
4. *Inconsistent Language:* If people don't use a common vocabulary, with clear and simple definitions of each word, they will waste valuable time trying to understand each other.
5. *Poor Issue Transparency:* If people do not feel safe raising issues, they will bury problems that will hinder progress toward their goals.
6. *Insufficient Resources:* If people try to do their work without the right resources, they'll end up with disappointing results.
7. *Inadequate Tools/Skills:* If people lack the skills and the tools they need to get desired results, they won't get the results.

NOW solutions, listed in Table 2.2, will help managers avoid committing each of the seven sins and thereby avoid all the waste that so often occurs when variation creeps into a management system. (Note: The parenthetical numbers in the "NOW SOLUTIONS" column in the table indicate the chapters in which you will find these tools).

From Declining to Improving Results

"All I need is a $79 Makita drill I can pick up at COSTCO," test technician "Eric Crane" complains to "Skip Manoj," his boss at Floating Point Systems.

Manoj hands Crane a two-page form it will take 15 minutes to complete.

Crumpling the paper in his fist, Crane murmurs, "Yeah, yeah, I know I can fill out a stupid purchase requisition form and get the drill from purchasing. They'll pay $154 for the same drill and it'll take three weeks. I need it now, Skip."

"I'm sorry. Some of the rules don't make sense to me either," Manoj consoles the younger man. "But that's how we do things around here. Trust me, there must be a good reason for it."

Always a top performer, Crane hates all the bureaucratic nonsense, but just shrugs his shoulders and walks away. One more pebble has been added to his growing mountain of frustration.

TABLE 2.2   NOW Solutions to the Seven Deadly Sins of Management

No.	Sins	Waste	NOW Solutions/Chapters
1	Unclear Direction	Lost Opportunities	Shared Vision/11; NOW Fundamentals Map, mission, key goals, values, outcome and process measures/5; NOW Breakthrough Map/6
2	No Line of Sight	Bad Choices	NOW Fundamentals Map, core processes and cascaded process measures/5; NOW Breakthrough Map/6
3	Unclear Accountability	Inconsistent Actions	NOW Inside/5, 7; Cascaded process measures/5; Quarterly Target Reviews/7
4	Inconsistent Language	Confusion and Misunderstanding	Detailed common language for everything from fundamentals to planning to problem solving/all chapters; Everyone knows it, talks it, and walks it/10
5	Poor Issue Transparency	Fear and Secrecy	NOW Inside/5, Seven; Quarterly Target Reviews/7; Seven-Step Problem Solving, Fundamental Improvement Plans/8; Breakthrough Status Reviews/6, 7
6	Inappropriate Resources	Disappointing Results	Breakthrough Planning/6; Outcome and process scorecards/5; Quarterly Target Reviews/7, Breakthrough Status Reviews/6
7	Inadequate Tools/Skills	Mission Failure	Core process knowledge accumulation/5; Seven-Step Problem Solving, Fundamental Improvement Plans/8; Breakthrough Planning/6

A typical manufacturing company wastes 25 to 30 percent of its operating budget on nonvalue-added work; service organizations waste 30 to 40 percent; and government wastes a whopping 40 to 50 percent. If you think those numbers have declined in the wake of the different management fads that have come along in the past 30 years, think again.

Results Decline   THEN   NOW   Results Improve

FIGURE 2.4   Results Improve in the Now

The problem stems, more than anything else, from management's inability to shift its approach to problem solving in a way that matches the shift from the old world of mass production to the new world of mass customization. That's why we focus too intently on how, where, and when people in organizations make decisions.

When a decision gets kicked upstairs to a higher authority, the full reality of the situation gets lost, and it will take far too much time for the decision to travel back to the front line for implementation (see Figure 2.4).

Consider this typical THEN chain of events:

1. Front-line worker encounters a customer problem.
2. Policy dictates that it go up the food chain to the employee's supervisor.
3. Supervisor cannot deal with the problem right away.
4. Supervisor must escalate the problem further up the food chain to a senior manager.
5. Decision travels back down the food chain, from senior manager to supervisor to front-line worker.
6. Front-line worker needs to ask some questions about implementing the decision.
7. Questions go back up the food chain.
8. Answers come back down two days later.
9. Impatient customer flees to competitor.

These impediments and time-wasters can be eliminated. When it comes to responding to a customer need, common sense would prefer a different flow of decision making:

1. Front-line worker encounters a customer problem.
2. Front-line worker runs through the organization's problem-solving protocol.
3. Customer receives a decision within an hour—if not immediately.
4. Customer remains loyal and tells 10 friends about the satisfying experience.

Typically, managers shoulder a lot of upper-level responsibilities and longer-term objectives, such as serving on task forces, planning for new products, taking compliance training, tracking budgets, and analyzing the situation when things go wrong. Responding to in-the-moment problem solving and decision making, unfortunately, can easily become an interruption to an already jammed schedule of higher priority work.

Meanwhile, front-line workers, who believe they lack the authority to act, can only watch helplessly as opportunity after opportunity slips through their fingers. Employees disengage. They feel, in the extreme, they have no choice but to let common sense fly out the window. "I'll just keep my head down and my mouth shut, and stay out of trouble."

The NOW solution enables the people who deal directly with the opportunities and obstacles to act with speed and precision. With it, managers:

- ◆ Create context.
- ◆ Train people in problem solving.
- ◆ Get out of the way.

Once solutions are offered swiftly, everyone wins: Customers get quick answers, front-line workers gain tremendous satisfaction, managers can focus on their strategic responsibilities, and the organization gets terrific results.

The Right Tools in the Right Place at the Right Time

Not long ago we at Mass Ingenuity were hired by the CEO of "InvestCo," a multibillion-dollar financial services company to help jump-start the company's poor performance. Somehow, its adoption of state-of-the art process improvement techniques had not affected the numbers at all. When I sat down with "David," one of InvestCo's key officers, I asked to see the binder in which he stored information on all of the company's process improvement efforts over the past year. David was a highly capable, bright, and enthusiastic man who really loved his job.

"Look at this," he beamed, as he showed me documents in the four-inch binder detailing the first major project.

| Management Tries Latest Fads to Fix Things | THEN ◄ NOW | Tools and Skills Enhance Management Direction |

FIGURE 2.5 Using Tools and Skills over Following Fads

It all looked impressive, so I asked, "What measurable improvements did the team achieve?"

David responded, "Well, since these were the first process improvement projects InvestCo implemented, we didn't want to put pressure on the employees by measuring results."

For the process to work, David and the team involved would have had to start by assessing the current performance and identifying what was getting in the way of *desired* performance (root cause), and then design solutions, implement them, and, finally, measure progress.

Nothing measured, nothing improved. David had invested a lot of time and enthusiasm in the project but had merely been going through the motions. Our report to senior management concluded: "No wonder you guys gave David that little office across from the boiler room. You wanted to install the latest fad, but your heart was never in it."

As illustrated in Figure 2.5, an overwhelming assortment of management tools and techniques has come along in recent years. But in too many cases, management merely tacks bells and whistles to a broken tricycle.

A NOW Management System builds a new tricycle. It prioritizes, connects, enables, and drives the execution of all work in an organization, ensuring that people enjoy the authority to use every resource to achieve the organization's goals. It can incorporate all the best and latest management tools, but only after leaders have established the right context, trained employees to solve problems, and then let them do their work without management interference.

From Disengaged to Engaged

It is Brad's job to assemble the cabinets his company, "FactorY," buys to house its supercomputers. But for the past four months the supplier has sent cabinets with the wrong fastening bolts, causing Brad to waste a lot of time finding the right ones and swapping out the bad ones.

Brad has been putting up with this because he has no place to go to deal with it—his boss, Maria, is too busy. Consequently, Brad has started to dread his work.

Fortunately, Brad gets a new boss, Mika. Soon after he arrives on the scene, he suggests to Brad to e-mail a quick explanation of his problem to Tammy, in Purchasing.

Brad sends his message, ending with, "Can you straighten this out?" Voila! The next shipment of cabinets comes with the right bolts. Brad can't believe it. "Thanks," he tells his boss. Mika pats his shoulder, and says, "Whenever you see a problem like this, go straight to the person who can help solve it. You don't need to ask my permission or fill out a bunch of forms."

Brad's former boss, Maria, was mired in the then. He and his buddies in the mechanical assembly department had nicknamed her the "Idea Pit" (Figure 2.6). Over time, they just let problems like the bad bolts slide, as they labored to deal with them without her help.

Maria herself would have preferred to solve problems more swiftly, but whenever she had tried to buck the system, her boss had warned, "Don't reinvent the wheel, Maria. We do things the way we do them for very good reasons."

All too many organizations lack a formal protocol for acting on opportunities and solving problems, even seemingly obvious ones like bad bolts. Why? *Boundaries*. Whether you realize it or not, your

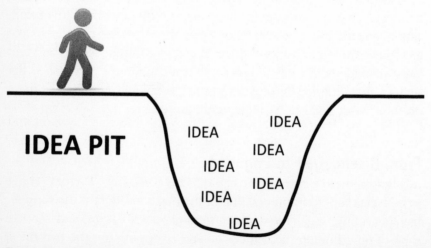

FIGURE 2.6　Idea Pit

management system prescribes what people can and can't do. It sets certain boundaries people cannot cross, even if doing so will solve, rather than cause, a problem. (Chapters 5 through 8 provide solutions to these issues.) In a THEN environment, a boundary erects a barrier to action. In a NOW workplace, it fades away when a problem needs an immediate solution. A NOW organization sets aside the notion of boundaries in favor of *striking the right balance between freedom and order* (more on this in Chapter 9). Without a means to solve problems whenever and wherever they arise, problems go unsolved.

We conducted a poll on LinkedIn asking the question "What percent of employee ideas get implemented in your company?" The results were discouraging. A full 81 percent of those responding said less than 10 percent of their employees' ideas ever see the light of day.

Leaders and managers need to rethink their definition of "employee engagement" (Figure 2.7). In the past, most leaders thought of it in terms of creating an environment where people felt valued and properly rewarded for their accomplishments. But you must go further. You must:

♦ Enable people to conceive and implement incremental improvements, microinventions, and microingenuity on their own initiative and without seeking permission.

♦ Make sure people understand the context created by the numbers that measure enhanced customer experiences, accelerated revenue growth, and reduced costs.

♦ Emphasize the added value of creating superior products and services produced at the lowest possible relative cost that command the best relative prices in the marketplace.

Employee engagement is not about people feeling all warm and fuzzy; it is about people possessing the knowledge, skills, and authority to act swiftly and skillfully without waiting for permission.

Workforce Engagement Declines THEN NOW **Workforce Engagement Improves**

FIGURE **2.7** Engagement Grows in the Now

Workforce Engagement

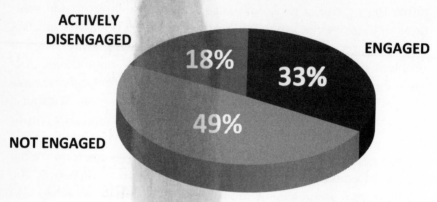

SOURCE: Gallup Consulting

FIGURE **2.8**   Worker Engagement Levels

According to The Gallup Organization and numerous other respected analysts, most enterprises fail at engaging their people in that way, and as a result end up paying an enormous price for that failure (see Figure 2.8).

No greater condemnation exists for conventional management practices than the disengagement of 67 percent of American employees. Of those, 49 percent couldn't care less. They just show up, follow orders, question nothing, and keep their mouths (and their brains) shut. The remaining 18 percent actively sabotage the company's performance.

The not engaged are the B and C players who do just enough to get by and win a decent performance appraisal. Knowing the system resists new ideas and prompt action, they go along to get along. They may work hard, but at 5:00 they punch out and stop thinking about their jobs the minute they walk out the door.

Actively disengaged people quietly throw monkey wrenches in the works, some of them small and relatively harmless, others big enough to bring the machinery to a grinding halt.

Recent research reveals the staggering cost of employee disengagement (see Figure 2.9). The Gallup Organization has published

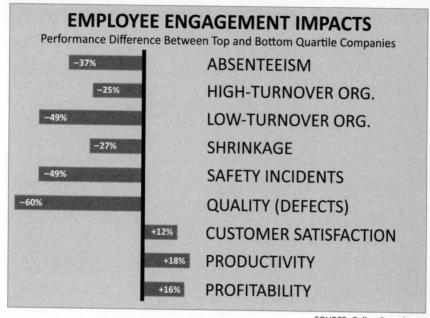

SOURCE: Gallup Consulting

FIGURE **2.9** The High Price of Worker Disengagement

the compelling correlations it found between levels of engagement and other seemingly disconnected factors. Companies in the top quartile of engagement (highest levels as rated by their employees) enjoy lower absenteeism and turnover rates, less shrinkage, fewer accidents, and fewer product defects, in addition to higher levels of customer satisfaction, productivity, and profitability. High engagement companies outperform low engagement companies in every one of these dimensions.

Obviously, if you want to improve the performance of your organization, you should spend time thinking about and enhancing employee engagement.

Fear plays a leading role in the drama of employee disengagement. Dr. W. Edwards Deming, the man largely credited for Japan's economic recovery following World War II, and its eventual climb to manufacturing preeminence in the 1980s, cited fear as the predominant force in the vast majority of businesses. Many leaders and managers rely on it. But fear has a way of creating dissatisfaction, disengagement, and even rebellion.

While the world of organizational life in which we function today may seem bafflingly complex, in many ways, the more complex it gets, the simpler it becomes. Rather than trying to micromanage all the countless variables you cannot control, you only manage the one you can control: the people who work in your organization and who can come up with the ideas that, cumulatively, will create and sustain your competitive advantage. One microingenuity plus one more micro-ingenuity, plus hundreds more equals *mass ingenuity*. And mass ingenuity equals market dominance.

Few modern organizations—with the notable exceptions of Amazon, Facebook, Disney, Nike, Apple, and a handful of others—come close to Google's reputation for innovation. Stories of Google's creative culture abound, from free meals to no dress code. One intern praised the company as "unconventional, one of the few places where you can be truly yourself." To emphasize its belief in freewheeling creativity Google established its TechTalks program, which brings world-renowned speakers to the Googleplex. Presenters have included a Nobel laureate speaking on creativity, and a monk describing "The Role of Spiritual Practice in the Modern World."

Fulfilling its stated mission, "making information universally accessible," Google not only has raced past its competitors to become a preferred supplier of computer services for hundreds of millions of people, it has also created a workplace where its people are fully engaged in accomplishing its mission.

■ ■ ■

Complete the Speedometer for Making the Shift to Now (Table 2.3) and add your net score to the summary sheet in the Appendix.

TABLE **2.3**   NOW Speedometer 2: Making the Shift to Now

Then	−1	0	+1	Now
We do not know exactly where we want the business to go				We all understand the company's mission, vision, values, and key goals
We do not connect what people do with our organization's direction				We connect every individual to the organization's direction
We do not hold everyone accountable for results				We hold everyone accountable for results
We do not use a common language to talk about our business				We use a common language to talk about our business
We avoid or hide problems				We never avoid or hide problems
We try to accomplish our goals without sufficient resources				We allocate sufficient resources to accomplish our goals
We lack the skills and tools needed to accomplish our goals				We always acquire the skills and tools we need to accomplish our goals
Subtotals				

Making the Shift to Now **NET SCORE**

Add this score to the consolidated score in the Appendix.

THEN | NOW

−7 −6 −5 −4 −3 −2 −1 |0| +1 +2 +3 +4 +5 +6 +7

3

Seizing the NOW Opportunity

Drive Growth with Yes

A shley pined daily for what she thought of as her perfect accessory. No, she didn't really need the pale blue Locman Italy 161 wristwatch, but she sure did want it. It would pair beautifully with her marine-blue jersey dress. And she had just two days to come up with a plan before she swept into the Neptune Society Charity Ball this Friday night. Even with online fashion retailer Zappos offering the timepiece on its www.6pm.com discount website at 71 percent off (dropping it to a mere $1,004.81), it was still just too expensive. Ashley couldn't justify the purchase, not on her PR account coordinator's salary. Then, at 1:10 in the morning Tuesday, Ashley's best friend Jenny texted her with the incredible news that 6pm.com had slashed the price of the watch to $49.95. Ashley clapped her hands in delight. "This is unbelievable!"

Bolting out of bed, her heart racing, Ashley punched the numbers into her smartphone and soon found herself waiting impatiently for the confirmation that she had snagged the last available watch. A minute later, confirmation arrived. "Yes!" shouted Ashley, pumping her fist in the air.

Midmorning the next day, Ashley received another text from Jenny, this one with a link to a Zappos' blog titled "6pm.com Pricing Mistake." Oh, my God! Ashley's heart sank as she read: ". . . this morning, we made a big mistake in our pricing engine that capped everything on the site at $49.95. The mistake started at midnight and went until around 6:00 AM PST. When we figured out the mistake was happening, we had to shut down the site until we got the pricing problem fixed." Ashley grimly prepared for her disappointment.

Then she read on: "While we're sure this was a great deal for customers, it was inadvertent, and we took a big loss (over $1.6 million—ouch) selling so many items so far under cost. However, it was our mistake. We will be honoring all purchases that took place on 6pm.com during our mess-up. We apologize to anyone that was confused and/or frustrated during our little hiccup, and thank you all for being such great customers. We hope you continue to Shop. Save. Smile. At 6pm.com. Signed, Aaron Magness, Director of Brand Marketing & Business Development for Zappos." Ashley smiled. She *had* saved, and she would, indeed, continue to shop at Zappos.

Zappos instantly and effectively solved what could have turned into a customer service nightmare, with hundreds of buyers vowing never to do business with the company again. Instead, Zappos immediately took accountability for the situation. During the 6pm.com pricing incident Zappos lived up to one of its "family" values: "Build open and honest relationships through communication." Later in his message to customers, Magness explained that although company policy did not require Zappos to honor the erroneous prices, the company would do the right thing and take the hit. Zappos also honored another of its company values: "Pursue growth and learning." No Zappos employee lost his or her job over the error.

You must, of course, do the big things well, getting the right products to the right markets at the right time at the right price. But in the age of speed, you must also do all the small things well. Zappos does it all well. With a sterling reputation for service, and boasting a unique corporate culture, the company grew from a start-up in 1999 to a billion dollars in revenue by 2008. Zappos sustains its competitive edge over agile competitors because its people, no matter how large or small their responsibilities, engage in improving the customer experience, driving growth and reducing costs. Sure, mistakes will happen. They always do. But those fumbles make everyone smarter.

When You Operate in the Now

On June 1, 2009, General Motors filed for protection under section 363 of Chapter 11, Title 11 of the United States Code in the Manhattan New York federal bankruptcy court. It was the result of a disastrous turn of events for a corporation whose revenues at one time would have made it the sixth largest economy in the world.

How could such a powerhouse have fallen so far?

While everyone knows about many of GM's problems, such as its failure to match Japanese auto manufacturers' quality, and the burden of huge costs related to labor union contracts, not many observers have written about one contributing factor that, as much as any other, toppled the once-dominant auto giant: its inability to keep pace with the transformation of the United States economy from its mass production roots to the new world of mass customization. In a world demanding now, General Motors lost significant market share because it could not overcome its history as a *then* company.

In 2009, GM had yielded its dominance of the global market to Toyota. You can trace Toyota's acceleration all the way back to the day in 1969 when Toyota shipped the first Corolla, soon to take over as America's favorite small car, to the United States, followed quickly by small pickups that earned a strong reputation for reliability and durability. Ironically, the first Toyota built in the United States, in 1985, rolled off the assembly line at the New United Motor Manufacturing (NUMMI) facility in Fremont, California, the result of a joint venture with General Motors. In the end, it all came down to which company turned the most new ideas into better products produced at lower costs. Already operating in the now in the early 1980s, Toyota was implementing more than 70 ideas per employee per year compared to 1 every 7 years per employee at General Motors (see Figure 3.1).

Does this mean that Japanese workers were smarter than their American counterparts, or that they were hungrier for success and rebuilding their country after World War II? Did Toyota's management install bigger suggestion boxes in its plants? Did they empty them more often in order to keep ideas from disappearing into the idea pit? Or does something else account for the fact that new ideas flourished at Toyota?

IBM's THINK program in the 1960s provides an example of the power of ideas. One of my colleagues told me a story about his

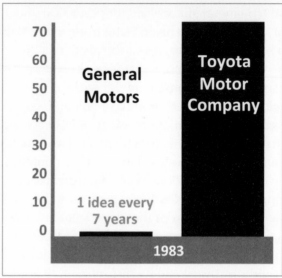

FIGURE **3.1**   Idea Implementation at Toyota and GM

summer job during his college years back in 1966, when he worked at IBM's Greencastle, Indiana, card manufacturing plant. "On every wall you'd see these THINK signs," Michael recalls. "It never meant much to me until I attended a company meeting toward the end of the summer when the plant's manager handed out bonuses to employees whose ideas the company had implemented. The size of the check reflected a percentage of the increased productivity or cost savings the idea produced for IBM worldwide." While the bonus may seem to be the point, the freedom to implement improvements was the core of the program.

Michael describes the standing ovation that erupted in the room when a punch machine operator went to the front of the room to collect a check for $25,000, a large amount of money today, a huge amount in those days. "Walt was a Korean vet and a farmer who could fix a John Deere tractor with a safety pin. He hated the fact that at the end of every shift we threw away half of the U.S. Treasury checks we had printed and punched with serial numbers because the punch machine constantly went off-register. He had found a way to insert a little spring in the punch machine that would keep it from going haywire every 20 minutes." A simple idea from a simple man solved a complex problem for a giant corporation. Walt saw a need and met it. Had IBM not sought out and rewarded ideas, a costly waste problem would have gone unsolved.

Business opportunities come and go every day. Many go unnoticed. But, increasingly, the key to success hinges on solving every problem and seizing every opportunity, whether one as seemingly inconsequential as adding a free case to a disgruntled customer's smartphone order with a personal note or as momentous as swallowing a whopping pricing error. If you don't do it, your competitor will. Does your customer express a need? Meet the need or miss the opportunity. Now you see it, now you don't.

The Toyota versus General Motors battle illustrates a causal phenomenon. Toyota's system of management *causes* it to respond to countless improvement ideas. Toyota's system enables its people to work in the now. Until recently GM, like most organizations, simply could not respond to the high volumes of ideas because they processed all of the input centrally. Any central processing of ideas automatically creates a bottleneck, unless the organization allocates sufficient central resources to process all of its idea input within a reasonable amount of time.

A close examination of idea processing in a centralized THEN system reveals that the organization passes all ideas through two filters: economic and political. "What return can we expect if we invest in this idea? What will the boss think of it?" Imagine all of an organization's ideas poised above a funnel (see Figure 3.2). No matter how large the hopper at the top, the hole though which the ideas must travel remains the same size. Each idea must pass through the two filters. At a practical level, an organization can allocate only limited resources to idea processing, which means it can only process a limited number of ideas. Thus the system will emphasize "big" ideas that will garner the highest ROI and win the boss's approval.

In this sort of system, key decision makers consider all the ideas and approve the ones they like best. An idea that will save $50,000 gets attention; the smaller ideas usually do not, for simple economic reasons. If implementation requires the approval and help of another department, then the idea must travel through that department's funnel as well.

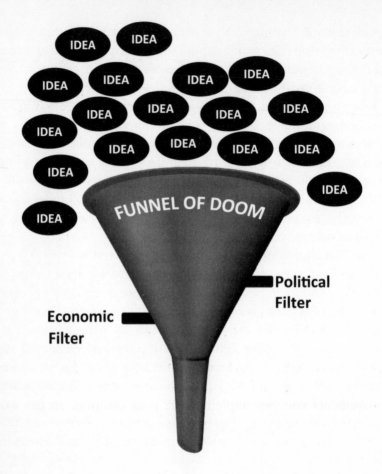

FIGURE 3.2   Funnel of Doom

Suppose you work on a customer service team and have just come up with an idea that will save $1 per routine incoming service call by eliminating one "For A, Press X" step in the process. When you finally get an audience with the decision maker in your organization, you could easily wait for 10 minutes while she puts out a staffing fire and answers a call from an angry customer who has demanded to speak to a supervisor. It's likely she would love to implement the idea, but if it depends on her having time, the idea will end up stuck in the Funnel of Doom.

In reality, your little $1 idea really *would* save the department a ton of time and money. In fact, it's not a little $1 idea at all; it's a $64,000 whopper! How? The innovation you propose, eliminating one un-necessary step in the service call process, will save $1 per call 20 times a day for each of the 12 people who answer calls over a 260-day period, resulting in $64,000 annual savings this year and next year and the year after that until the end of time. Your little molehill of an idea has morphed into a mountain.

How many other "little" ideas have been accumulating in inboxes across organizations? Do the math: If an organization employs 100 people and implements an average of one $1 idea per employee per year that has an annual savings of a mere $1,000 each, the organization can add $100,000 to the bottom line. It's an exponential equation with astonishing results. Just consider what happens when you move from one $1 idea (each saving $1,000 annually) to 10 such ideas per employee per year. Don't forget Toyota's 70 ideas per employee per year (see Table 3.1).

Unless you find a way to give little ideas a chance, you may be stunting your business's growth and compromising your profit margins. Growth depends on quickly recognizing and acting on every opportunity to reduce costs and improve the customer experience, accomplishments that relate directly to the number of incremental improvements you can implement in your business. In the world of *now*, the next big thing may be a seemingly really small thing. Think big but act on the little things that can pay big dividends.

TABLE 3.1 The Power of the Little Idea

		Assumes Each Idea Implemented Saves $1,000				
		Number of Employees				
		10	100	1,000	10,000	100,000
IDEAS IMPLEMENTED PER EMPLOYEE	1	10,000	100,000	1,000,000	10,000,000	100,000,000
	10	100,000	1,000,000	10,000,000	100,000,000	1,000,000,000
	25	250,000	2,500,000	25,000,000	250,000,000	2,500,000,000
	50	500,000	5,000,000	50,000,000	500,000,000	5,000,000,000
	75	750,000	7,500,000	75,000,000	750,000,000	7,500,000,000
	100	1,000,000	10,000,000	100,000,000	1,000,000,000	10,000,000,000

While $1,000 savings may sound like a lot, you can easily achieve it in a frequently repeated process. You only need to repeat a process that saves $1 each time three times a day for it to result in annual savings of $1,000.

To Try or to Do, That Is the Question

We often tell clients a fable of two companies: Trying, Inc. and Doing, Inc. Both companies set their sights on bringing a new Talking Teddy to market. Dick, the CEO of Trying, and Jane, the CEO of Doing, meet for lunch. "How's it going with the Talking Teddy project?" Jane asks Dick. "Oh," Dick replies, straightening his tie, "We've been getting a lot of opinions from all our people about it, we've been spit-balling a lot of plans, I've let people know they can experiment with anything that strikes their fancy, I take 100 percent of accountability for getting the product to market, but I'd say we're about 10 months behind our original schedule. You know me; I like to keep those creative juices flowing. How about you?"

Jane reaches into her oversized handbag and pulls out a 12-inch-high fuzzy brown teddy bear, which she sets on the table. "Hello," she says to the bear. The bear swivels its head and pipes up in a squeaky voice, "Howdy, Jane. I'll have the toast and honey, please."

Dick's eyes widen. "Wow! When will you start selling that thing?" Jane chuckles, "We expect to ship 10,000 the day after we announce it to the media tomorrow."

How did that happen? How did Doing, Inc. manage to beat Trying, Inc. to market? As Jane explains it, "We run a pretty tight ship. I know all about the loosey-goosey style of management, but I've found we can actually be far more creative with structure and discipline. We demand facts over fiction. We draw up detailed, written plans. We use tight timelines to drive our creativity to practical solutions. We stress managed and coordinated execution, we hold *everyone* accountable for results, and we usually hit or beat our numbers."

Compare, for instance, how the two companies solved the interactive voice-activation problem with their prototype products. Dick's people spent a lot of time pursuing what they called "out of the box" ideas that honored Dick's mandate to "loosen up, let the creative juices flow, don't dismiss any new idea." This approach led them down a lot of unproductive rabbit holes. Jane's people, on the other hand, tackled the problem methodically and quickly found a way to license a proven voice-activation system to meet their needs. They focused on results, delivering a great new product, on time, and within a reasonable well-defined budget.

TABLE 3.2 Trying versus Doing

	Trying	Doing
	Casual and Inconsistent	**Disciplined and Structured**
Thinking	Opinion-Based	Fact-Based
Planning	High-Level and Unstructured	Detailed and Written
Execution	Informal	Managed and Coordinated
Accountability	With Manager	Public
Results	Unpredictable and Disappointing	Predictable and Positive

The moral of the story? *The road to failure is paved with the broken promises of trying; the path to success is built with the solid results.*

Doing organizations use discipline and structure to get results. Facts, not hunches, drive their thinking. They devise detailed, written plans; they carefully coordinate execution of those plans; and they always hold every stakeholder accountable for results. These habits give them both the will and the skill to succeed in a fiercely competitive world where doing the right things and doing them quickly makes all the difference between merely trying and actually doing (see Table 3.2).

Trying organizations prefer to operate informally, varying their approach from initiative to initiative. They respect hunches and often base their decisions on opinion and persuasion. They formulate their plans at the highest level and restrict accountability to one-on-one relationships between managers and subordinates. They move at glacial speed.

One of our clients, Permanente Dental Associates (the dentists of Kaiser Health Plan), asked us to help them solve a big problem. On average, it took 6.7 weeks from eligibility for subscribers to get their first appointment. Those who endured this wait ended up expressing great satisfaction with their treatment. Those who lost patience went elsewhere. Over an 11-year period, Kaiser and Permanente Dental Associates had launched 10 documented initiatives to address the issue, but none had resulted in measurable improvement, a classic trying symptom. New health-plan subscribers complained so bitterly that, before long, the group benefit insurance brokers in the region became reluctant to sell Kaiser's dental plan to their clients because they didn't want to deal with the initial complaints.

Our consultants helped Dr. John Snyder and the leadership of the Dental Program for Kaiser, create a charter for a Breakthrough Team (a methodology detailed in Chapter 6). They assembled a cross-functional team to tackle the project by recruiting sponsorship and participation from the two unions representing the support staff and the dental assistants and hygienists, and following a structured methodology, we guided the team through a process of gathering facts about the problem and nailing down the root causes. During the process the organization formulated a Shared Vision (details in Chapter 11), which became instrumental in the ultimate success of the initiative. One dramatic change that was implemented involved redesigning the annual off-site retreat attended by 600-plus employees to include an afternoon dedicated to serving new subscribers. Employees turned it into a positive, festive internal competition, measuring not only how many new members they pulled through the process that afternoon, but how highly new members rated their satisfaction with respect to this first experience with Kaiser dental services. In the end, elapsed time from first contact to first appointment dropped from 6.7 weeks to 2.7.

In the case of the competition between Dick and Jane to get the talking bear to market, when the team Dick had assigned to the voice activation problem ran up exorbitant costs without getting within spitting distance of a solution, Dick fired the team leader. Jane, on the other hand, dealt with the lack of progress by sitting down with her team, deliberately exploring the obstacles that were getting in their way, and helping them quickly draw up a detailed plan to attack the problem.

The 9 Rules of Then, the 11 Rules of Now

Then companies that play by all the old rules suffer lackluster performance and pay a heavy long-term price for their ways. The Now companies break the old rules, formulate new ones, and enjoy the fruits of their success.

The people who work at then companies suffer under the 9 Rules of Then, as illustrated in Figure 3.3.

Fortunately, corporate Robin Hoods break those rules and replace them with more enriching ones. Leaders like Microsoft's Bill Gates,

The 9 Rules of THEN

- Follow orders even when they make no sense.

- Keep your mouth shut and your opinions to yourself.

- Please your boss because he/she controls your future.

- Do not challenge management or you will be labeled a troublemaker.

- Blame others when things go wrong.

- Do not waste company time on social media.

- Punch the clock and leave your work at the office.

- Never complain, never explain, except after work.

- Say no to customers who demand an exception to company policy.

FIGURE 3.3 The 9 Rules of Then

Apple's Steve Jobs, Google's Larry Page and Sergey Brin, Starbucks's Howard Schultz, Amazon's Jeff Bezos, cookie maker Debbie Fields, Zappos founder Tony Hsieh, Nike's Phil Knight, and Intel's cofounder Andy Grove rewrote the rules, creating vibrant organizations capable of sustaining innovation (ideas) and execution (Doing).

The 11 Rules of NOW

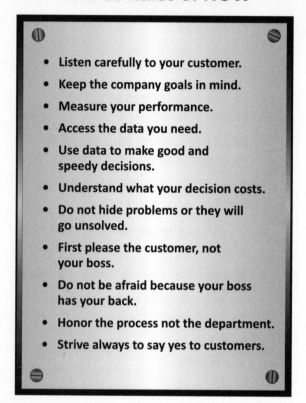

- Listen carefully to your customer.
- Keep the company goals in mind.
- Measure your performance.
- Access the data you need.
- Use data to make good and speedy decisions.
- Understand what your decision costs.
- Do not hide problems or they will go unsolved.
- First please the customer, not your boss.
- Do not be afraid because your boss has your back.
- Honor the process not the department.
- Strive always to say yes to customers.

FIGURE 3.4   The 11 Rules of Now

Success in the now demands a new set of rules geared to the era of mass customization. The 11 Rules of Now, enumerated in Figure 3.4, set forth the basic new rules that enable every employee to act on every opportunity every time.

Simon Says and Mother, May I?

"Before I implement the change," assembly associate Jayar Bonifacio told me, "I want to share with you what I have done." Jayar and I were working for Floating Point Systems, where I was running manufacturing.

Jayar had uncovered a problem that was delaying the circuit board assembly process. Hell-bent on reducing throughput of the two-sided,

4,000-component circuit boards by 25 percent, he knew he would need to prove that his idea would work. After systematically collecting and analyzing data and developing a potential solution to the problem, he came to me with clipboard in hand.

"John, I suggest we implement this change tomorrow, because it'll reduce the time it takes to build a board from four days to three." He spoke with the confidence of a person who has compelling data to back him up.

"Have you validated your solution with manufacturing engineering and purchasing to make sure it's correct?" I asked.

"Of course, they've signed off on the change, and we're ready to go tomorrow."

As it turned out, Jayar had pinpointed the root cause of a costly problem. The plant had been "baking" its circuit boards for years, applying vicelike pressure and high heat to ensure the boards would not warp later in the assembly process when assemblers added the components and ran the whole shebang through the wave solder machine. We did that because a warped board turns into a $25,000 piece of scrap. However, Jayar proved that the step was completely unnecessary by validating the supplier's claim that its engineers had solved the warping problem a year earlier. While purchasing and manufacturing engineering knew the supplier claimed to have solved the problem, no one had taken time to validate it. Stopping the baking not only sped production of the board, it reduced the cost by eliminating the labor and expense of the process. How did it happen? One enthusiastic front-line worker skillfully stepped up to the plate without needing anyone's permission to solve a problem.

At the survival level we invent ingenious ways to fend off an enemy, snag a fish, or fetch an apple from the top of a tree. The creative act unites our passion to make something happen, our joy when we apply best thinking, and our enjoyment of the fruit of our most skillful actions. Humans instinctively want to improve their lot in life. Throughout humankind's existence individuals and groups have constantly endeavored to make their lives more secure and fulfilled, whether in terms of food and shelter or of such intangibles as happiness, freedom, and love. All along the way obstacles and problems have always cropped up to thwart progress, but the human spirit unfailingly strives to conquer whatever impediments it encounters.

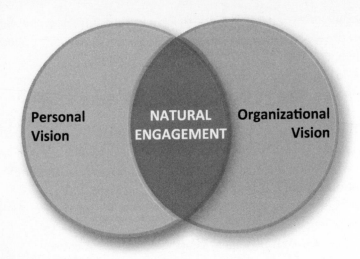

FIGURE 3.5   Natural Engagement

But something strange happens on the way to work. Bright, ambitious people climb out of bed when the alarm clock goes off on Monday morning, shower and eat breakfast, then head for work with all of their native creativity in tow, only to arrive in a workplace where far too often management effectively tells them to sit down, shut up, and just do their jobs.

Organizations create visions of their future and spend a lot of time crafting mission statements. While employees rarely write down their personal mission statements, they do envision successful futures for themselves. When their personal visions connect to the organization's vision, they naturally engage in making it all come true (see Figure 3.5).

Shifting Gears to the Now

After the bombs of World War II stopped falling on Japan, and the combatants signed the Articles of Surrender on the *USS Missouri* in Tokyo, a lanky, rumpled U.S. professor arrived in the shattered country. He came to help it rebuild its economy and reverse its image as a producer of cheap, shoddy junk. Enlisted by General Douglas MacArthur, the supreme commander of the Allied powers, Dr. W. Edwards Deming initially came to Japan in 1947 to help engineer a census of Japan's population; but before long, his expertise in statistical process control prompted an invitation for him to speak to the Japanese Union of Scientists and Engineers.

By 1950, Deming was training hundreds of Japanese engineers, managers, and scholars every year. He had failed to gain any traction in the United States. Most American businesspeople dismissed his strange thinking about management. In Japan, however, his efforts culminated in establishment of the Deming Prize, still awarded annually to the best-run company in Japan. Prize winners over the years include Toyota, Nippon Electric, NEC, Komatsu, Bridgestone, Fuji Photo, Mitsubishi, Nissan, and Sanyo. Dr. Deming's teachings to the Japanese businessmen who ardently followed him catapulted Japan's economy to the third most productive in the world today (behind the United States and the People's Republic of China).

Deming looked at a business as a complex system consisting of many parts. That view led to statistical process control (the foundation of Six Sigma), a new approach to organizational psychology, the end of old-school management by objectives, and a refreshing emphasis on "constancy of purpose." Deming's philosophy and teachings continue to influence current management practices around the world.

The three gears that power the NOW philosophy of management owe a great debt to Deming's ideas. He lectured vigorously about two of the three NOW gears. *Eliminate fear* ranked number 8 among his 14 key principles for transforming business competitiveness while *reduce variation* ranked number 5. The third gear, added in Figure 3.6, is *pursue constraints*.

When all three of these gears mesh together fluidly, they help an organization engage its people, reduce its costs, and focus on the greatest opportunities.

ELIMINATE FEAR

Fear within an organization causes people to freeze, flee, or fight. In the workplace it can lead to inaction, resignation, or rebellion. It prevents employees from improving the work they do. It keeps them from putting their expertise, experience, knowledge, and passion to work seizing opportunities and solving problems. If they feel they will receive criticism or retribution for acting on their instinct for

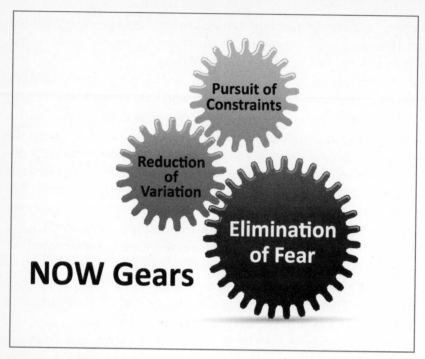

Figure 3.6   NOW Gears

improvement, they may avoid taking the initiative to do what it takes to contribute to the organization's growth and well-being.

As Roger Connors and Tom Smith point out in their classic book on accountability, *The Oz Principle: Getting Results Through Individual and Organizational Accountability,* far too many managers use accountability as a club because they have never learned a more positive definition. Connors and Smith make clear that such an approach to accountability builds a wall of fear that actually inhibits people from getting results. True accountability, they argue, arises when management creates an environment where every employee seizes every opportunity to "See It, Own It, Solve It and Do It."

Toyota's employees couldn't possibly have implemented those 70 incremental improvements if every time they wanted to take action they ran smack into the wall of fear. For them to make and act on ideas, they needed to feel safe. The NOW organization replaces the old wall of fear with a safe environment where people do not hesitate to offer suggestions, take initiative, and question the status quo. In Chapter 9, we will look at specific ways to create such an environment.

REDUCE VARIATION

The concept of variation comes from the field of statistics and provides the basis for Six Sigma and process control efforts. You can also apply it to the management process itself.

In the natural world, variation occurs all the time: No two snowflakes or fingerprints look exactly alike, no two people feel the same level of passion about their work, and no two managers operate precisely the same way. Those variations occur within a standard range that results in a bell-shaped curve. If you examine a sufficient number of physical objects (snowflakes and fingertips), qualitative experiences (customer service encounters), or leaders (anyone who manages anything), you will find a predictable range of performance. That's perfectly normal. In the case of process control, the more you tighten the range of variation, the more predictable the process becomes. The more predictable it becomes, the less intervention it will require. Recall the punch machine operator at the IBM plant. When the company implemented his invention worldwide, it reduced variation in the output of the card-punching machines, which now required much less adjustment and produced a lot less waste. Whenever you can achieve higher-quality output (meaning it more consistently falls within a tight range), the more efficient the process becomes. It costs less and produces less waste (see Figure 3.7). In the case of a customer service process, when you more consistently and predictably delight your customer, the less time and money it will cost you to operate that process. Imagine how much time, energy, costs, and customer goodwill Zappos would have lost had it not honored the pricing on its website.

The same applies to management. If you define management's job as picking a direction from point A to point Z and aligning all necessary resources in that direction, then the better management does that job, the more efficiently the organization will achieve the desired results. Getting there will cost less money and waste less time. Think back to the Seven Deadly Sins of Management discussed in Chapter 2. Chalk them all up to variation in the management process.

REDUCE VARIATION

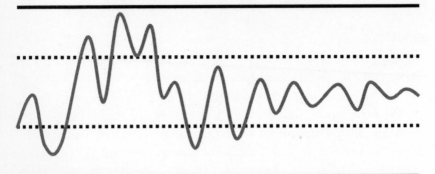

When any work you do goes poorly, it consumes unplanned resources.

FIGURE **3.7**   Reducing Variation to Minimize Waste

Can you think of a more essential management task than reducing or eliminating all that variation?

In general, you can measure organizational performance in terms of the variation that occurs in all of its processes, from idea development to production, marketing and sales, and customer service. The NOW organization reduces variation across the organization. Otherwise, all of the variation in its processes will slow it down and cost it dearly. Most importantly, it will keep it from making the transition from trying to doing, from *then* to *now*.

PURSUE CONSTRAINTS

Simply put, a constraint is anything that restricts the organization from achieving its goals. While a wide range of constraints in the form of rules, policies, procedures, accepted practices, and even beliefs may hamper business processes, the Theory of Constraints draws your focus to the biggest obstruction, or the *primary constraint*. To get your organization on the shortest path to improvement you must pursue elimination of primary constraints (see Figure 3.8). You can find primary constraints in all processes in all organizations, and whether it's the management process of planning or the human resources process of hiring or the manufacturing process of fashioning new products, the overall organization is only as capable as its weakest link.

PURSUE CONSTRAINTS

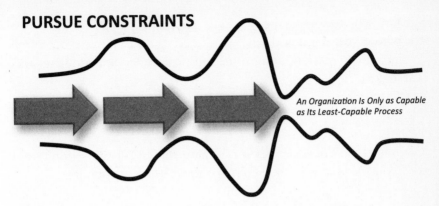

An Organization Is Only as Capable as Its Least-Capable Process

Figure 3.8   In Pursuit of Constraints to Eliminate Bottlenecks

If "Acme Finance" processes home mortgage loans, and the credit checking department can process 10 loans a day, the income verification department can process 3 a day, the department that verifies home values 8 a day, and the department that checks everyone else's work 6 a day, Acme cannot process more than 3 loans a day. The income verification process places a primary constraint on the whole system. If you want to speed up loan processing, you must remove that constraint. If you increase the income verification process to seven a day, then you find yourself addressing a new primary constraint: the process that checks everyone's work.

NOW businesses grow and become more productive and profitable because they systematically pursue and eliminate their primary constraints.

When you lead a large organization, you can apply the same concept to the macro-level processes of the organization. If marketing isn't generating enough qualified leads for sales to hit its targets, then lead generation is the primary constraint. If service cannot keep up with demand for support because the business is growing so rapidly that customer wait times are increasing to the point that sales drop, service is the constraint.

Success in a NOW world requires an unprecedented level of execution, a level seen commonly in Doing companies. As a manager you can't afford to leave the details to chance as Trying companies usually do.

On which road have you put your company? To get a feel for where you stand and what you need to do to move more surely in the right direction, administer the next NOW Speedometer (see Table 3.3).

■ ■ ■

Complete the Speedometer for Seizing the NOW Opportunity and add your net score to the summary sheet in the Appendix.

TABLE 3.3 NOW Speedometer 3: Seizing the NOW Opportunity

Then	−1	0	+1	Now
We implement very few of our employees' ideas				We implement most if not all of our employees' ideas
We are a TRYING organization				We are a DOING organization
We live by the 9 Rules of Then				We live by the 11 Rules of Now
We see most employee ideas as half-baked				Our employees skillfully implement their own ideas
We use fear to get people to do their jobs				We work hard to eliminate fear
We don't apply the concept of variation to management processes				We seek to reduce variation in our management processes
We allocate resources regardless of complaints				We allocate resources based on constraints
Subtotals				
The NOW Opportunity NET SCORE				

Add this score to the consolidated score in the Appendix.

SPEEDOMETER

THEN		NOW
−7 −6 −5 −4 −3 −2 −1	0	+1 +2 +3 +4 +5 +6 +7

4

Leveraging the NOW Game Changers

Gain the Speed You Need

Sameer Bhatia, a Silcon Valley gaming entrepreneur, and Vinay Chakravarthy, a recent graduate of Boston University Medical School, faced a serious illness and an uncertain future. Both young men were diagnosed with a deadly form of leukemia. They needed a life-saving bone marrow transplant. A suitable match for both men required donors of South Asian ancestry. That reality gave them a 1-in-20,000 chance of success, a considerably bleaker prospect than for the population at large.

With only weeks to find the right matches, their tech-savvy friends came to their rescue, bringing a millennial mind-set, social media, and cloud computing to the task. In 48 hours they had reached 35,000 people.

How?

First, they established two "brands": HelpSameer.org and HelpVinay.org. Then they developed a NOW strategy to promote them. They built phone directories and trees, set up conference bridges, created videos, and erected a donor platform using Web 2.0 cloud tools. They launched a viral campaign in the form of an e-mail blast to 100 of Sameer's close friends, asking them to expand the movement by contacting their own close friends. The campaign exploded globally via Facebook, blogs, and YouTube.

TABLE **4.1**   Game Changers and the Need for Speed

Game Changer	How It Drives to Now
Social Media	Enables instant real-time, two-way communications
Cloud Computing	Enables more efficient, lower-risk automation of business processes and quicker responses to customers' immediate needs
Millennial Mind-Set	Holds little regard for hierarchy, desires instant gratification, and does not tolerate anything that moves at a snail's pace

During the next 12-week period, the group conducted 470 bone marrow drives, engaged 3,500 volunteers, generated more than 150,000 website visits, created 1 million-plus media impressions, and registered 24,611 new South Asian bone marrow donors.

The campaign succeeded in finding matches for both men, who continually blogged their experiences to the world. And yet, despite a courageous battle, Sameer died three months after his transplant. Vinay, relapsing after his successful transplant, died three months after Sameer.

This sad ending did not draw the story to a close, however. The campaign located enough new potential donors to give a greater hope of survival to more than 250 South Asians in desperate need of bone marrow transplants.

The same three game changers, which are reshaping the business landscape in revolutionary ways (as illustrated in Table 4.1), can enable action in any organization.

Satisfying the Hunger for Instant Information

On the television screen a dark shadow obscured the face of tweeter @BPGlobalPR. His voice altered to protect his identity, he told an ABC television interviewer that he had launched a Twitter campaign against British Petroleum over its handling of the 2010 Deepwater Horizon Gulf of Mexico oil spill.

"Well," he explained, "I did it just as a reaction to the way BP was trying to spin things in the Gulf." This man's tweets led followers to believe he actually worked for BP, when in fact he was satirizing BP's actions in the Gulf. "I felt they were trying to protect their brand more than they were trying to be proactive and honest about the situation down there."

Within a week, the satirist had acquired more than 180,000 followers, far surpassing the real BP's measly 18,000. His efforts embarrassed the petroleum giant, who eventually could not get away with "spinning" the story in a way that underplayed its magnitude and severity.

Josh Simpson, the then-26-year-old Los Angeles comedian who engineered the campaign, demonstrated the power of social media to keep an organization honest, no matter how many social media messages the organization itself sent out.

Consider these telltale signs of the impact of social media:

♦ "I learned more about my daughters from their Facebook pages than I did from raising them," claims Bob Iger, CEO of the Walt Disney Company.

♦ According to Morgan Stanley's Internet Mobile Report, in July 2009, the number of monthly social media users surpassed the number of e-mail users.

♦ Bank of America now responds to 1,100 tweets per day with its staff of "Twitter Agents."

♦ Facebook adds 700,000 new members and processes 45 million updates every day.

♦ Bloggers post enough content each and every day of the week to fill 7,000 issues of the *New York Times*.

♦ Wikipedia, launched in 2001, now offers 15 million free articles in 200 languages, contributed by 1 million volunteer authors.

Social media is changing the face of the world because it provides free and instant access to everything we want, from people and relationships to facts to photos and videos to ideas and thoughts to a place to share our deepest conviction—to just about anything we dream about, including the darker sides of life.

At the time of this writing, more than a billion people access the more popular social media sites (Figure 4.1), such as Facebook, Twitter, LinkedIn, Flickr, Yammer, Foursquare, and the more specialized sites, such as Academia.edu (for academics and researchers), Bigadda (Indian social networking site), BlackPlanet (African American), Habbo (for teens), Mixi (Japan), Muxlim (Muslims), Ozone (mainland China), and Vampirefreaks.com (gothic and industrial subculture).

FIGURE **4.1** Social Media Logos

Brian Solis, author of *ENGAGE! The Complete Guide for Brands and Businesses to Build, Cultivate, and Measure Success in the New Web*, and one of the most thoughtful and prominent analysts on the subject, argues that the phenomenon has predicted the end of "business as usual."

"We are trying to take an existing one-to-many approach and adapt it to a mass customization world, and it just doesn't work," believes Solis. In no small part, the fundamental challenge and opportunity for businesspeople centers around the fact that social media incorporates two-way communication, and the resulting "conversation" switches organizational communication from a one-way, one-to-many broadcast strategy to a two-way thoroughfare for creating relationships. Old-school THEN corporate communications delivered impersonal pronouncements from on high. The new-school NOW tools force organizations to engage with human beings and to listen as much as they talk (see Figure 4.2).

Ford Motor Company's head of social media Scott Monty employs social media to give his company a human face in the marketplace. Monty humanizes his messages. He mixes his real life with his passion for Ford, the company, its products, and its people, expressing the company's beliefs and its efforts on behalf of its customers, its employees, and the world. Monty freely offers social media advice and commentary on his personal blog at www.scottmonty.com where his posting ranges from strategic advice to sharing a haiku he wrote about Ford and a new product.

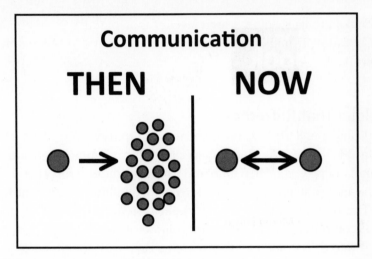

FIGURE 4.2   THEN versus NOW Communication

Solis applauds that sort of corporate communication. Executives should approach human conversations enthusiastically, because everyone responds warmly about subjects that matter to them. Besides, Solis says, the conversation will occur, whether you like it or not. "The conversation was going on and they just weren't hearing it," Solis points out. "The common misperception is that social media invented the conversation, the ability to speak to one another. All it does is vocalize, amplify, and visualize sentiment, and that is the point. It tells you something, something you need to hear."

Social media exposes all of an organization's problems and challenges. That can be scary, but it can also supply a much-needed dose of reality therapy. Solis, who advises many global corporations, has seen social media not only raise customer service issues, reveal product development and product marketing opportunities, lay wide open human resource or finance problems and opportunities, but also provide a vehicle for dealing with those issues in the now.

Companies can also harness the power of social media within their own walls. An employee who has worked too long in a broken process completely disengages, silently doing the work without complaining, so the process stays broken. Using social media, that same employee can reveal his concerns and frustrations without fear of penalty. Management hears a human voice, and the process gets fixed (more on this topic in Chapter 8).

Social media sustains a high level of transparency in an organization because it drags ideas and opportunities and problems to the forefront.

A Cloud That Refreshes

The British retail giant Sainsbury's new CEO, Justin King, took a huge hit in 2005 when he decided to scrap the mammoth information technology project he had inherited from his predecessor. That painful but necessary step cost the company a $526 million investment write-off. The new automated supply chain system functioned so poorly that it could not handle the sheer volume of merchandise customers had ordered. So much of that merchandise had gotten stuck in the company's depots that Sainsbury had to hire 3,000 extra stocking clerks to fill backed-up orders.

A press release from Sainsbury associated with the write-off summed up the calamity: "IT systems have also failed to deliver the anticipated increase in productivity, and the costs today are a greater proportion of sales than they were four years ago. The rollout of future systems and upgrades has been slowed down while focusing on driving benefits from the systems already in place." Translated, that corporate doublespeak meant, "Sainsbury will go back to using some of its old manual processes."

With the failure of its investment in custom technology, Sainsbury joined a rather large club.

As Jeff Atwood points out on the website Coding Horror: "The failures [of information technology initiatives] are universally un-prejudiced: they happen in every country; to large companies and small; in commercial, nonprofit, and governmental organizations; and without regard to status or reputation. The business and societal costs of these failures—in terms of wasted taxpayer and shareholder dollars, as well as investments that can't be made—are now well into the billions of dollars a year."

In its 2009 CHAOS report surveying 400 organizations, the Boston-based Standish Group concluded that respondents considered a scant 32 percent of IT projects successful, 24 percent outright failures (cancelled before completion or delivered but subsequently abandoned), and 44 percent "challenged" (see Figure 4.3).

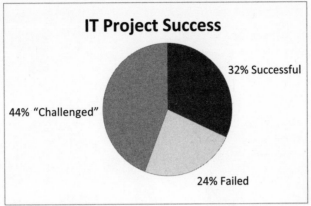

SOURCE: Standish Group

Figure 4.3 IT Project Success Rates

Initiatives that fail to deliver on the promise of better, faster, and cheaper drive business leaders crazy. They cannot afford the cost of failure and breaches in security. They feel frustrated by the complexity of do-it-yourself IT, all of which has led to a flourishing IT project rescue industry. Sir Peter Davis, Sainsbury's CEO before Justin King, was forced to quit, partly over his compensation, but no doubt also over his failure to stop the firm's slide into third place, even after investing 3 billion pounds in infrastructure.

Cloud computing offers a wonderful alternative to such home-grown failures. It can eliminate much of the complexity of major IT projects, reduce the risk of failure (even the huge Amazon failures in April of 2011), and fulfill the promise of better, faster, and cheaper (see Figure 4.4).

Wikipedia defines cloud computing simply as: "Internet-based computing, whereby shared resources, software, and information are provided to computers and other devices on demand, as with the electricity grid."

A comparison of Microsoft's Outlook and Google Apps offers a good example of conventional versus cloud computing. For the IT department of "Thunderhead, Inc." to make Outlook (e-mail, calendar, contacts, and task management) available to its employees, IT must place and maintain copies of the application on every single computer and smart device throughout the organization, and it must also install a centralized set of exchange servers to host Thunderhead's

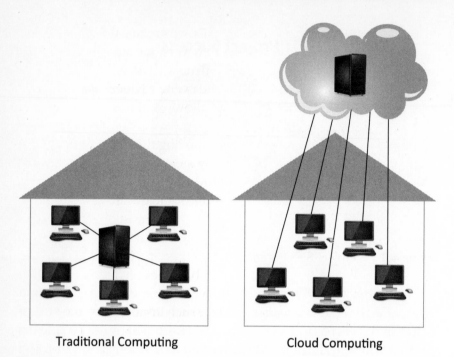

Traditional Computing   Cloud Computing

FIGURE 4.4   Cloud Computing versus Traditional Computing

reliance on Outlook. Whenever Thunderhead decides to update to a new version of the application, or deal with a change in the software, someone from IT must "touch" every user (whether that means going to the location of each computer or reaching out electronically) and solve every problem generated by the transition. This explains why many organizations keep running Office 2003, many years and multiple new versions later. Installation, maintenance, and support for a new but basically similar system not only consumes a lot of staff time, it also breeds complexity and costs an arm and a leg.

Compare that approach to the cloud alternative adopted by "Lightning, Inc." Lightning has switched from Outlook to Google Apps (at least as rich in capability as Outlook), which Google maintains on its own servers in its data centers, allowing Lightning to access it on the internet. Lightning switched the whole company from Outlook to Google easily and instantly. Google took care of it. Now, suppose that Lightning acquires "Raindrop, Inc." and its 500 people, who have been using Outlook. Lightning can perform the switch in a single day, without ordering new servers, loading new software, or even transferring files. Downstream, the firm will no longer need to fret over upgrades, new versions, and add-on applications. Google will take care of all that, with an additional bonus: Google charges less than Microsoft and even provides free service for small businesses—if they agree to allow unobtrusive ads to run alongside the applications.

While many businesspeople fear moving their data to the cloud because cyberbandits can more easily steal it, they really need not worry about that because the big cloud providers (Google, Amazon, Salesforce, and even Microsoft, IBM, and Oracle) can invest far more resources in security talent and tools than most businesses can afford. According to the Ponemon Institute, data breaches cost a company about $204 per violated customer. When the institute evaluated 45 case studies of major breaches, it found that they cost on average $6.7 million each, with one company spending a whopping $31 million to deal with one such instance. A secure cloud can drastically reduce the likelihood of such losses. The big cloud players can afford the best security.

Salesforce.com has provided cloud-based Customer Relationship Management (CRM) for many. In fact, today, Salesforce.com handles the sales data for some 82,400 customers, including Wells Fargo, Cisco, Google, Starbucks, and Japan Post. Its Force.com application offers a powerful "mashup" of CRM capability and social media, transforming CRM from an inside tool into an integrated customer-interfacing platform. A mashup mixes together numerous cloud applications to create a complete solution. Force.com claims its mashup solution runs five times faster at about half the cost of traditional, noncloud-based solutions. In the cloud you can connect and leverage multiple tools. You layer an identity management engine from Avatier Corporation onto a blog tool such as WordPress, and then connect the combination to an online shopping engine such as Amazon. From the customer's perspective, the integrated tools feel natural and seamless. A client organization pays per use when it relies on a Software as a Service (SaaS) model, where it need not buy and customize a big application with its own blog, its own identity management, and its own online store.

According to IDC Research, customers opting for Force.com enjoy 76 to 85 percent cost reductions in terms of traditional labor costs for a new CRM, 76 percent reductions in the cost of development cycles, and a 75 percent drop in the time it takes to make upgrades and improvements. Japan Post reported saving $10 million from its transition to Force.com over what it would have paid for a conventional new system. While the financial savings appeal to clients, Salesforce claims its alternative also represents a far better ecological solution, measured in terms of grams of CO_2 emissions per transaction (1.35 grams per transaction for on-premises transactions, 0.2 for Google Apps, and .03 for Salesforce.com).

Mike Hoefer, VP of software engineering for CA Technologies, a $4 billion IT management software and solutions company, explained his decision to move his company's computing to the cloud: "We've been building our own platforms for years, and we recognized that keeping them on the premises and hosting them and paying for all the infrastructural costs and ongoing labor, etc., etc., makes zero sense. We evaluated it a lot and came back to Salesforce—specifically, Force.com—as the most stable, the most feature-filled, the most we could trust."

The cloud offers solutions to many of the problems businesses face as they attempt to leverage technology to improve performance. It may not offer a perfect panacea, but it can help any alert organization create and sustain a competitive edge in a world that increasingly demands mass customization.

The Power of Millennial Thinking

At Harvard, an unauthorized website of student photos went up one weekend and quickly became so popular that by Monday morning traffic had overwhelmed and shut down the school's servers. On February 4, 2004, Harvard student Mark Zuckerberg relaunched the website from his dorm room, under the name "The Photo Address Book." Eventually, students simply called it "The Facebook." By the summer of 2010, Mark's site counted 500 million active users, 70 percent outside the United States, and had created a net worth just shy of $7 billion for the young entrepreneur.

"When you give everyone a voice, and give people power, the system usually ends up in a really good place," Zuckerberg has said. "So, what we view our role as, is giving people that power."

TABLE **4.2** Generations and the Events That Shaped Them

Generation	Born	Memorable Events
World War II	1928–1945	The war, McCarthyism, economic expansion
Baby Boomer	1946–1953	Assassinations of Martin Luther King, Jr. and John and Robert Kennedy, Vietnam, civil rights unrest, women's liberation movement, walk on the moon
Boomer Cohort 2	1954–1965	Watergate, Nixon's resignation, raging inflation, gasoline shortages
Generation X	1964–1980	*Challenger*, Iran-Contra, Reaganomics, AIDS, MTV, Star Wars, fall of the Berlin Wall, Desert Storm
Millennial (Gen Y)	1976–2004	September 11 attack, Afghanistan and Iraq wars, war on terror, global financial crisis, and the Great Recession

SOURCE: Wikipedia

Zuckerberg's millennial generation, born between the mid-1970s and the year 2004, goes by many other names: generation Y, generation next, generation why, the trophy kids, echo boomers, or the net generation. In many ways Zuckerberg symbolizes the generation's naive optimism, love of technology, and commitment to social good. This generation brings a whole new set of skills and attitudes to the workplace. They also present some perplexing problems to their managers and senior colleagues. While experts don't agree on their precise birthdates, they do agree on the events that shaped them, enumerated in Table 4.2.

In her book *Y in the Workplace: Managing the "Me First" Generation,* Dr. Nicole Lipkin, a psychologist who also holds an MBA, describes what she sees as the five big shifts that shaped the millennial mind-set.

Parenting Shift: Their parents replaced the old adage that "children should be seen, not heard" with "the sun rises and sets on our children's wants and needs." As a result, this generation disdains hierarchy and authority.

Education Shift: Their teachers focused on building their self-esteem, giving each child a gold star for his or her work, regardless of its quality. "Every kid's a winner" dominated educational philosophy. If a child failed, blame it on the teacher. As a result, millennials do not respond well to poor performance reviews and do not follow the motto that guides their older colleagues: "If you do not succeed, try and try and try again." They also display weak critical thinking skills, because their education stressed self-esteem over knowledge.

Global Shift: Constant access to media heralding bad news from all corners of the earth has stimulated this generation to demand the rewards of life. Earlier generations experienced crises, from the assassination of John F. Kennedy to the war in Vietnam and the Watergate scandal, but this new generation sees the world falling apart and they do not want to invest and make sacrifices today for rewards tomorrow. As a result, they exhibit a general impatience and want to get ahead and enjoy the fruits of their labor instantly.

Technology Shift: The first generation born with a keyboard in their hands, the millennials have never experienced a world without constant and immediate access to anything and everything that interests them. They feel at home in a world of 140-character sound bites. As a result, they do not suffer anything that moves slowly, especially in organizational life.

Socialization Shift: In the world of Twitter, MySpace, and Face-book, this generation counts its "friends" in the thousands. They connect with others, and they keep connected with people they've never actually met face-to-face and with countless others they probably never will meet. As a result, they possess a tolerance of a wide range of people, regardless of age or generation or race or creed, and can build and willingly sustain more, and more varied, relationships than their seniors can even imagine.

These fundamental shifts have forged a mind-set that offers both pluses and minuses when the millennials enter the workplace. Recently, while chatting with the managing partner and several of his top-level colleagues at a regional accounting firm, I saw the extreme frustration on their faces as they struggled to figure out how to integrate the fresh graduates they were hiring into the firm. Accounting firms rely on young, smart, ambitious, hard-working graduates to do the bulk of all the down-and-dirty audit work. But this generation is seeking an alternative to long hours at a desk, resists the notion of paying dues to make partner, and does not respond to negative feedback. It was obvious to these partners that their entire business model is at risk; yet facing the reality that partner wages cannot be maintained if the young want-to-be CPAs aren't willing to put in the long hours at low pay was painful to them.

Dr. Lipkin suggests such managers pay attention to three major positives of the millennial generation:

Work/Life Integration: This generation seeks a more holistic approach to life. They do not want to damage their quality of life off the job by sacrificing themselves on the job for career success at any cost. They have seen the price their parents paid, and to them it is not worth it.

Social Responsibility: Whereas their elders pay a lot of lip service to business ethics and corporate social and environmental responsibility, this generation takes these ideas seriously. They believe that with power comes responsibility. They refuse to sit by and watch the behavior that toppled the Enrons of the world.

Innovative and Creative: Given their easy access to anything and everything, the millennials bring a high degree of inventiveness and creativity to the job. Change does not intimidate them. They have erased the term "status quo" from their vocabulary. At the same time these attributes offer a huge potential addition to the world of work, they stretch and alter organizational traditions and thinking.

Deep down, those frustrated senior accountants actually share many of the same beliefs with their young colleagues, from which they can find some middle ground and move forward. Who doesn't long for better work/life integration? Who doesn't feel outrage over the actions of British Petroleum, AIG, Enron, and the U.S. government in the wake of Katrina? And who enjoys working for a broken organization that has gotten mired in the status quo?

Success hinges on a leader's ability to integrate the positives of the millennial mind-set into the organization, while at the same time reducing the negatives.

If You Can't Beat 'Em, Join 'Em

On December 10, 2010, Chinese dissident Liu Xiaobo won the Nobel Peace Prize while serving an 11-year sentence for inciting subversion of state power. Prior to the announcement, the Chinese government blocked access to this information by its 1.3 billion citizens on all major global news sites on the internet. Try as it might, however, the government could not stop the news from reaching its people because 130 million Chinese use the country's popular Facebook-style site every day.

If you have not yet joined this unstoppable movement, you can start today, using these social media (SM), cloud computing (CC), and millennial mind-set (MM) tactics:

Social Media Tactics

SM 1: Read Brian Solis's book *ENGAGE!*

Solis demonstrates that social media don't just offer useful marketing and branding tools, they empower internal and external conversations that will shape your business, whether you like it or not. The conversations can make you feel good, but they can also show you the cracks that need repairing. All of them contribute to the transparency the millennial mind-set demands.

SM 2: Use LinkedIn, Facebook, and Twitter.

Given its focus on building business relationships, LinkedIn makes the most sense for beginners. The site offers tutorials on how to use the medium. Set a goal of forging 100 connections, then 200, then as many as you can handle, spending, say, 10 minutes a day on the project. Eventually, you can move on to other sites and then link them all together. The synergy among the sites will amaze you.

SM 3: Abandon the "no use of social media while at work" policy.

If you try to discourage employees from accessing social media at work, you'll only end up as frustrated as those Chinese officials who found they could not halt the flow of information. In his book, Solis shares a lot of eye-opening examples of successful policies from such organizations as Intel and IBM. They reveal how trusting your people to use social media in a thoughtful and responsible way can create an army of good cyberspace representatives.

SM 4: Develop and deploy an externally focused social media strategy.

It usually makes sense to get some professional help from a skilled consultant to help design a system for maintaining the needed conversations with your stakeholders. Even if you only manage a department and cannot implement a companywide initiative, you can launch a social media blog for your internal customers and suppliers. Basecamp offers easy-to-use tools for collaboration and initiatives, and WordPress is a simple blogging tool. The bigger your organization, the more critical external social media become. You are not looking for one-time marketing input but for a way to remain in constant touch with all the people who are essential to your business.

SM 5: Develop and deploy an internally focused social media strategy.

In Chapter 7, we'll discuss ways to use social media as a part of an integrated set of tools that enable action. Internally, social media allow access to the information needed to make prompt decisions. While they enable the sharing of ideas and suggestions, their real power lies in their capability to surface problems and solicit solutions.

Cloud Computing Tactics

CC 1: Read *Executive's Guide to Cloud Computing* by Eric A. Marks and Bob Lozano.

Don't leave it all to your IT people. Every leader should grasp the basic principles and applications of cloud computing. Marks and Lozano translate the complex subject into plain language, so their book will help you get quickly past the hype of vendors selling their patented cloud computing products and to a solid general understanding of the subject.

CC 2: Trust the cloud to keep your information safe.

Since you cannot guarantee the 100 percent safety of information in your on-premises systems, it makes sense to rely on the big cloud providers that can afford to hire the best world-class experts and employ the most cutting-edge state-of-the-art technologies to ensure data security.

CC 3: Take a baby step before you make a giant leap.

Pick a pilot project, small enough to manage easily but important enough to your business that you must pay attention to it. Try something like Google Apps (mail, contacts, and calendar), a fairly important shift, but a relatively minor and safe one. Or consider transporting your website hosting to Rackspace or a similar provider. You'll detect few if any changes besides reduced costs and fewer problems.

CC4: Let the cloud increase your employees' access to the data they need to make sound and swift NOW decisions.

In Chapter 7, we'll explore this topic in more detail. For now, just bear in mind that in order for your people to make great decisions in the now they need complete access to business data that will give them everything they need to make those decisions. When that happens, every decision advances your organization toward its goals.

CC 5: Create and implement a bold cloud strategy.

Your long-term strategy should aim to get your organization sufficiently out of the technology business so that you can concentrate more of your time and energy on your real business. This should become a major goal of your organization.

Millennial Mind-Set Tactics

MM 1: Read *Y in the Workplace: Managing the "Me First" Generation* by Dr. Nicole Lipkin.

You need to understand what makes this generation tick, and how their way of approaching and seeing the world will affect the workplace.

MM 2: Engage everyone in the effort to understand the millennial mind-set.

Initiate training, facilitate open conversations, and engage your millennials. Understanding what the millennials are looking for in the businesses they deal with can provide important insight into what your business will need to do in the future.

MM 3: Analyze the implications of the millennial mind-set on your organization.

Ask yourself some tough questions: What do we do that just won't fly in a millennial world? Do we have any business practices (causing environmental harm, using cheap offshore labor with poor working conditions, providing unfair rates of pay and unsafe work environment, etc.) that, if exposed, could put our business at risk? Does our business count on any traditional approaches to getting the job done (exhausting hours, uncomfortable working conditions, excessive travel, etc.) that repel young talent? Do we welcome ideas and input from our most junior colleagues?

MM 4: Develop a game plan to minimize your risks and fill the gaps.

If your business model demands you hire fresh graduates, and expects them to pay their dues in the form of low wages and long hours and months on the road (like our accounting firm friends), then you probably need to rethink that model. While less populous than the baby boomer generation, these new recruits will exert proportionally greater influence on the corporate world. You need them. Develop a new approach to recruiting, nurturing, rewarding, and retaining their talent.

MM 5: Welcome the millennial mind-set as the new reality.

It's not unusual to meet executives who simply shrug their shoulders and dismiss the millennials as a bunch of spoiled brats. Whether you like it or not, the new kids on the block will end up running the show. Use them or lose them. Abuse them, and your more forward-looking rivals will harness their talent to leapfrog over you. It's your choice.

Implement most or all of these tactics, and you will move your organization more surely into the now. The full transition will take time, of course, but you should be able to measure some positive effects right away.

■ ■ ■

Complete the Speedometer for the Leveraging the NOW Game Changers (Table 4.3) and add your net score to the summary sheet in the Appendix.

TABLE **4.3**   NOW Speedometer 4: The NOW Game Changers

Then	–1	0	+1	Now
We seldom discuss social media in our organization				We study social media to understand how to use it more effectively
We have developed no external social media strategy				We have adopted an effective external social media strategy
We do not use social media inside our organization				We use social media a lot inside our organization
We do not rely on cloud computing at all				We keep moving toward cloud computing solutions
We do not include cloud computing in our technology strategy				We have designed an aggressive cloud computing strategy
We do not understand the millennials				We understand and benefit from what the millennials offer
We do not include the millennial mind-set in our business strategies				We fully incorporate the millennial mind-set in our business strategies
Subtotals				

The NOW Game Changers **NET SCORE**

Add this score to the consolidated score in the Appendix.

		THEN		NOW		
–7 –6 –5 –4 –3 –2 –1	0	+1 +2 +3 +4 +5 +6 +7

Working in the NOW Business

Create the Context for Speed

With two outs in the bottom of the ninth inning, the "Spokane Bears" were clinging to a one-run lead over the "Bellingham Tigers" in the Washington State high school championship. With bases loaded and a full count on the opposing batter, the Bears' pitcher, "Matt Struthers," peers at the catcher's signal. Instead of the expected knowing nod, he shoots the catcher a puzzled look. Still, he begins his windup.

The Bears' coach, "Pat Atkinson," sensing confusion about the called pitch, yells, "Time out!" and begins a leisurely stroll from the dugout. When he reaches the mound, he looks his pitcher square in the eye. "Did you see the signal?"

"Yes, Coach," Struthers quickly replies.

Atkinson returns to the dugout and watches as Struthers again stares at the catcher's mitt as if trying to solve a complex differential equation.

"Time out," yells Atkinson again. The umpire shoots Atkinson a scolding look as the coach now jogs to the mound.

"Did you *see* the signal?" Coach Atkinson repeats, standing nose-to-nose with the nervous pitcher.

"Yes, Coach, I did." Struthers is crestfallen as his coach returns to the dugout. Sweating now, he prepares again to throw the most important pitch of the season. But something isn't right.

"Time out!" Atkinson calls once again as he bursts out of the dugout. The umpire scowls and pushes his mask atop his head.

Atkinson, taking the ball from his pitcher's hand and looking intently into the young man's eyes, demands, "Matt, do you *understand* the signal?"

"No, Coach, I don't!" Struthers finally admits.

"Just throw a high inside fastball. Alright?" Struthers nods his consent.

In the now, you cannot afford to miss crucial signals whether from teammates or the marketplace. The Era of Mass Customization does not permit confusion on the field of play. The game is on the line 24/7/365. The wrong move at the wrong time can cost you the inning, the inning can cost you the game, and the game can cost you the season. All employees need to know their roles in the game so when the signal comes they can immediately recognize it and act on it.

Context (clarity about direction, including mission, vision, values, key goals, and measures) sets the foundation for NOW work, and it is management's responsibility to create a culture that enables employees at all levels to act and communicate quickly. Context sets the stage on which employees make their decisions.

The best context provides answers to five key questions:

- Where are we going?
- What role do I play?
- How do I measure my success?
- How free am I to make decisions?
- How do I make the best possible decisions?

A cobbled-together, disconnected management system cannot create an effective context. Such a system might *accidentally* get you where you want to go, but one that you consciously and purposefully build to drive all of your organization's routine work will get you there faster.

Thinking in the Now

Whatever your business, whatever your goals, you must make sure that you and your people do the routine tasks, the day-to-day work, exceptionally well. You must have a powerful engine in place to drive your business. Far too often the engine an organization builds consists of an assortment of parts loosely cobbled together. When the funny noises start, managers reflexively begin taping on new parts and slapping on more glue to create an ever more complex Rube Goldberg–like contraption. It's a desperate attempt to make things run more smoothly, but, instead, it creaks and clatters and eventually breaks down. For the system to function like a well-oiled machine, you must make some scary and often gut-wrenching decisions. You must transfer authority for making decisions to the person who works at the point of action.

Since managers cannot be in all places at all times or deal with every problem or opportunity that pops up, it doesn't make sense to require every important decision to cross your desk. That's what THEN organizations do. NOW organizations, on the other hand, develop a new mind-set, one that starts at the top and permeates the entire organization.

The NOW Mindset
1. I use facts to find truth.
2. I serve my customers.
3. I improve my processes.
4. I count on people, people count on me.
5. I keep score to maintain focus.

FACTS REVEAL TRUTH

When a problem-solving team at Central Point Software looked into why the company was not shipping orders within the 48 hours it promised to its customers, what they uncovered shocked everyone. While most people assumed the problem lay with customer service and shipping, it turned out that the finance department's manual credit card approval process was creating a bottleneck in order fulfillment. Facts, it turned out, revealed the truth. Why had the facts proven so elusive? Although each employee understood the responsibilities of the role he or she filled, no one understood the entire process fully enough to identify the cause of the problem. Identifying the truth almost always requires both a bird's-eye view and a worm's-eye view of the situation. Most organizations, especially large ones, rely too heavily on faulty assumptions, inaccurate anecdotal evidence, and outdated conventions, rather than the complete and accurate details of the situation.

Leaders in NOW organizations require members of their team to gather facts and do research. They teach that *"I use facts to find truth."* They let people know they not only welcome, but also expect, the truth, no matter how detrimental or disappointing it may be.

Everyone Serves a Customer

For years the employees who worked in the final test department at the semiconductor equipment manufacturer Electro Scientific Industries (ESI) had to reinstall a camera that was in the complex laser-based product the company was selling. Why? The employees in the department that installed the camera initially kept setting the camera to display a "portrait" format, which the test department invariably needed to change to "landscape." This meant removing, rotating, and reinstalling the camera every time. Amazingly, the employees in the test department continued to go through this process for every camera, rather than discuss the problem with the supplying department.

As an executive on the management team of ESI, I introduced the concept that "whoever receives my work is my customer." If each function thinks of the other as its customer, it will spend more time getting to know one another's needs. Thinking of each other as a customer always improves the ability of all departments to move the organization toward its goals. That got the camera installers thinking about *their customer*: the test department. They initiated a conversation about what the customer thought of their service. Immediately, the problem with the camera installation surfaced. "Oh, we didn't know that. It'll be fixed tomorrow." Solving that problem quickly and effectively as soon as someone drew attention to it marked the beginning of a respectful relationship between the departments.

Traditionally, when problems arise in THEN organizations functional departments look *backward* to the supplying department, rather than *forward* to the department that receives the work. That dynamic promotes rather than resolves tension. Looking forward solves problems *before* they arise. Thus, the whole chain of customers benefits, especially those who matter most—the end users who buy the product.

Looking *forward* to the customer who receives your work sets in motion a systemic, constructive logic for driving the organizational improvement that is essential to doing *business at the speed of now*. It means constantly reminding yourself that you serve customers and you must meet their needs.

Work Is a Process

"Mary" always racks up exceptional numbers at the market research firm "EKnowledge," where her sales volume, customer satisfaction scores, and margin greatly exceed those of her peers. People admire Mary's gift of gab and cannot imagine anyone better suited for the job. If you ask her about it, she laughs, "Oh, I'm no Einstein. In fact, truth is, I'm kind of lazy. I don't like to waste my time doing things that don't work," she says in mock self-deprecation.

She goes on to explain: "I have this process I have fine-tuned over the past couple of years, and I have learned what works in each kind of situation I run into. When something doesn't work, I try something else until I find a way of handling customer objections in a way that removes their concerns and makes it easy to buy our service."

Mary views her work as a process, a series of interconnected steps she takes to satisfy customers. She constantly thinks about how she could improve a step in the process and thus enhance the customer experience. She never stops looking for opportunities; and when she spots one, she seizes it immediately. Thomas Edison, when asked if he ever got discouraged regarding his seemingly endless attempts to invent the lightbulb, said, "No, I just figured I had discovered a thousand ways not to make a lightbulb."

NOW organizations understand that work is not about a job description or the department you work in; it is about getting the work done efficiently and effectively. Customers don't care about departments; they just want their needs met, so process thinking also helps us break down the silos that distract everyone from the real work of improving processes (see Figure 5.1).

Every minute of every day, Mary and her colleagues tell themselves, *"I improve my processes."*

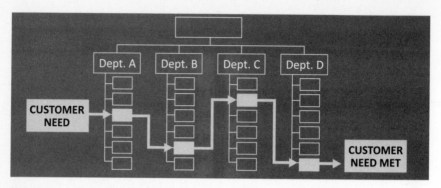

FIGURE 5.1   The Process of Work

PEERS INSPIRE ACCOUNTABILITY

Standard Insurance needed to solve a problem. The company's 14 account teams, spread across three regions, could not deliver necessary paperwork to new customers as promptly as they should. On-time delivery among the teams ranged from an impressive 90 percent to a dismal 10 percent. When two regions adopted the best practices of the team that was consistently delivering 90 percent or better, their numbers rapidly approached 80 percent on time, with steady progress toward a 90 percent target. The other region lagged far behind, with on-time delivery consistently running below 50 percent.

The vice president of the faltering region, rather than taking the best practices road, had chosen to reach the target her own way. If the facts proved that her approach wasn't working, why did she stubbornly persist with her approach? Because she did not want to change a paperwork process her people knew and liked. The other two regional vice presidents who had accomplished remarkable turnarounds with the best practices approach told me, "We're thinking of jumping on a plane and flying out to sit down with her and show her how this new approach works and why we think it makes sense. She's holding us all back from reaching our targets." But a funny thing happened when they called to schedule the trip. The stubborn vice president told them not to bother. She would make the change immediately. Within 30 days the combined on-time score for all regions exceeded 80 percent, and two months later it hit the 90 percent target.

How did that happen? Ms. Stubborn respected her peers, and that respect motivated her to take responsibility to fix her region.

When people know that others are counting on them, they feel inspired to meet their peers' expectations. Positive peer pressure can significantly boost individual motivation to set goals, take initiative, and get results. No matter what your job, you always bear in mind that, *"I count on people, people count on me."*

Scorekeeping Maintains Focus

Imagine you've taken a job that involves playing basketball 40 hours a week. Five days a week you go to the court and play as well as you can from 8:00 AM to 5:00 PM. You play hard, but no one ever keeps score. At the end of the year your manager sits you down for an annual performance review. What can she tell you but "You showed up and did your best"? Would you feel a sense of accomplishment? Would you enjoy hearing your manager say that to all the players, whether good, bad, or indifferent?

Let's change the dynamic: Management installs a scoreboard on the gym wall and divides the players into two well-matched teams. Now at the end of each hour or day or week or month, you and your team rate each other's performance and talk about specific ways each player might do even better. You'll focus, strive to improve, work on your technique, test new strategies, and go to work each day eager to play the game. With everyone fired up, the team will get better and better at its game.

Would anyone bother to play basketball or watch the Final Four on television if no one kept score? Like it or not, the world runs on scorekeeping. We all keep score in life. Scorekeeping gives us feedback, motivates us, and focuses our attention on getting results. "What gets measured gets done," is a popular quote often attributed to legendary management thinker Peter Drucker.

Effective scorekeeping for most work processes and business outcomes involve measuring three variables: cost, quality, and time (see Figure 5.2). To ensure optimal focus, managers must create a balance of measures that drive optimal behavior. They want their people to produce the right product on time and on budget. Failure in any of those dimensions betrays the customer. Ship a poor-quality wing nut, and it will come back. Replacing it will cost everyone time and money. Meanwhile, the customer, unwilling to absorb the cost of waiting for a good wing nut, defects to a competitor. It's a

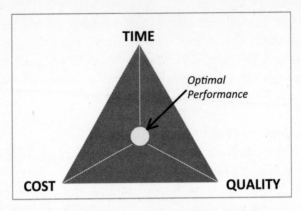

FIGURE 5.2   Scorekeeping Variables: Cost, Quality, and Time

lose-lose proposition. The same logic holds true in the department-to-department handoffs of normal work life.

THEN companies tend to use few measures, and the ones they do use often fail to keep the right scores. Take "performance against budget," for instance. This most-used and least-useful measure tells you nothing, except whether or not you spent the money you thought you would spend. But what does it tell you about whether or not you are making satisfactory progress toward your business goals? NOW company leaders want to know about that progress. They use scorekeeping to create the right context for action. The right context gives employees the maximum freedom to act in service of the customer. The right measures create the right context by clearly communicating what you expect your people to accomplish. Every good management system relies on them. They remind everyone, *"Keeping score helps maintain focus."*

Management Is a System

In 2001, Ken Schiller and Brian Nolen, owners of Rudy's Country Store & Bar-B-Q and Mighty Fine Burgers, Fries and Shakes of Austin and Round Rock, Texas, wanted to propel their eight-year-old business from good to extraordinary. To do that, they made a decision to adopt the Malcolm Baldrige National Quality Award framework, which provides comprehensive guidelines for running a business well.

The award, whose logo is shown in Figure 5.3, has been bestowed annually since 1987 by the president of the United States. It is the nation's highest presidential honor for performance

FIGURE **5.3** Baldrige Award Logo

excellence through innovation, improvement, and visionary leadership; its benchmarks can help any company improve, whether they apply for the award or not. In 2011 Schiller and Nolen did apply, and their commitment to excellence paid off when President Obama invited them to the White House to receive the 2010 Baldrige Award for small business.

The Baldrige framework, like Mass Ingenuity's NOW Management System, offers a systemic approach to management that enabled Schiller and Nolen to guide their 554-person, $37.5 million business to greatness. The results speak for themselves:

◆ Unit sales grew. They went from $3 million per store in 2000 to over $7 million in 2010.

◆ Business profits increased. Rudy's earned an increase of 47 percent average gross profits in 2010, and Mighty Fine earned 44 percent (compared to the 40 percent industry average).

◆ Customer satisfaction rose. Scores reached 4.7 on a scale of 1 to 5 (compared to 4 for their closest competitor).

◆ Turnover declined. They had 50 percent turnover for production workers, versus competitors' 85 percent, and absenteeism rates of 1 percent, compared to 5 percent for its closest competitor, all while offering comprehensive benefits to workers who put in 30 or more hours a week.

Schiller and Nolen made all this happen because they thought of management as a system they could continually improve. Managers rarely have the time to step back and assess whether the processes and systems they put in place years before still serve their purpose.

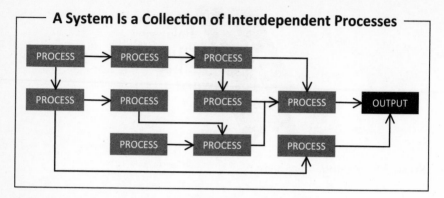

FIGURE 5.4   Interdependent Processes That Make Up a System

A system is a collection of interdependent processes that produces a result, as illustrated in Figure 5.4. You use a management system to get results in your business, whether you think about it that way or not. The more you *see* the management system and understand it, the more you can control it. If you don't control your system, you may be spending more time putting out fires than improving processes.

A well-designed management system continually adjusts resources in a way that moves the enterprise toward its goals as quickly as possible, with the least waste. No matter how well oiled the system, problems will always pop up, but an effective system will deal with each problem as quickly and efficiently as possible. When problems do arise, you must determine their relative importance, separating the urgent ones that require immediate attention from the smaller ones that don't. Remember how critical it is to identify, pursue, and remove constraints?

In 1990, Baker Boyer Bank, a well-run regional operation based in Walla Walla, Washington, embarked on an initiative to strengthen the business by mapping every single process in the organization. Unfortunately, the bank made one very common mistake: It treated all processes equally. All processes are not equal; and not all processes are equally problematic. When you set about redesigning your management system, you should never tackle the whole forest at once; you should, instead, seek out and deal with the problem trees first. Otherwise, you will spend a lot of time and money focusing on unnecessary work.

So what exactly should you do? First, start thinking in terms of the overall system. A system has a purpose, and the purpose of the system is to accomplish some sort of output or outcome. By concentrating on and clarifying your organization's mission, values, vision, key goals, and outcome measures, you gain the necessary bird's-eye perspective to set your system's purpose. For your system to deliver on its purpose, it must accomplish the mission within the context of your values and fulfill your vision through the measurable achievement of your key goals.

Baker Boyer Bank hired our consulting team to work closely with Megan Clubb, then executive vice president and now president and CEO of the organization. During the engagement we developed a tool we call the NOW Fundamentals Map (see examples, Figures 5.5 and 5.6). This tool helped the bank redirect its effort to map all of the bank's processes into a much more systemic approach to operating and improving the business. In particular, it helped the bank's leaders separate the truly troublesome processes from the ones that ran fairly well. That brought much needed focus to what really needed changing. By generating an overview of the organization, the bank was able to much more easily pinpoint its major constraints and then focus improvement efforts where it would yield the greatest return.

While most small regional banks have merged into bigger national chains, Baker Boyer Bank remains a thriving and highly respected independent player in its market. It remains focused, purposeful, and highly effective.

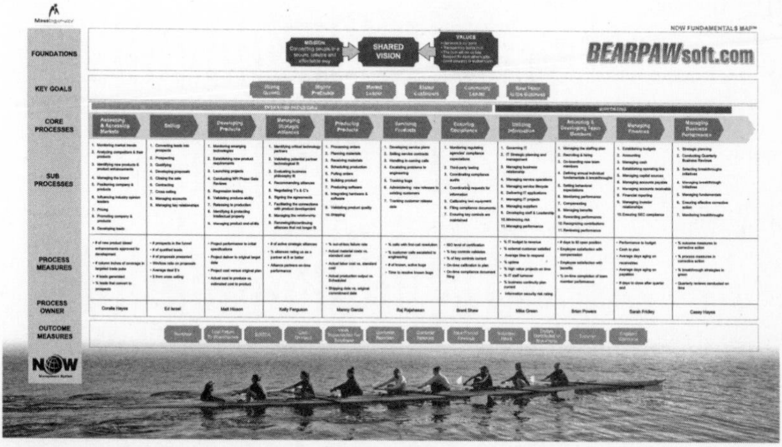

FIGURE 5.5   NOW Fundamental Map

Mass Ingenuity

BEARPAW/soft.com

FOUNDATIONS

MISSION — Connecting people in a secure, reliable and affordable way

→ **SHARED VISION** →

VALUES
- Our word is our bond
- Transparency builds trust
- The buck will stop here
- Passion for each other's growth
- Good stewards of Mother Earth

KEY GOALS

Strong Growth	Highly Profitable	Market Leader	Elated Customers	Community Leader	Best Team in the Business

CORE PROCESSES

OPERATING PROCESSES

Assessing & Accessing Markets	Selling	Developing Products	Managing Strategic Alliances	Producing Products	Servicing Products	Ensuring Compliance

SUPPORTING

Utilizing Information	Attracting & Developing Team Members	Managing Finances	Managing Business Performance

SUB PROCESSES

Assessing & Accessing Markets	Selling	Developing Products	Managing Strategic Alliances	Producing Products	Servicing Products	Ensuring Compliance	Utilizing Information	Attracting & Developing Team Members	Managing Finances	Managing Business Performance
1. Monitoring market trends	1. Converting leads into prospects	1. Monitoring emerging technologies	1. Identifying critical technology partners	1. Processing orders	1. Developing service plans	1. Monitoring regulating agencies' compliance expectations	1. Governing IT	1. Managing the staffing plan	1. Establishing budgets	1. Strategic planning
2. Analyzing competitors & their products	2. Prospecting	2. Establishing new product requirements	2. Validating potential partner technological fit	2. Planning	2. Selling service contracts	2. Third-party testing	2. IT Strategic planning and management	2. Recruiting & hiring	2. Accounting	2. Conducting Quarterly Business Reviews
3. Identifying new products & product enhancements	3. Qualifying	3. Launching projects	3. Evaluating business philosophy fit	3. Receiving materials	3. Handling in-coming calls	3. Coordinating compliance audits	3. Managing business relationship	3. On-boarding new team members	3. Managing cash	3. Selecting breakthrough initiatives
4. Managing the brand	4. Developing proposals	4. Conducting NPI Phase Gate Reviews	4. Recommending alliances	4. Scheduling production	4. Escalating problems to engineering	4. Coordinating requests for information	4. Managing service operations	4. Defining annual individual fundamentals & breakthroughs	4. Establishing operating line	4. Managing breakthrough initiatives
5. Positioning company & products	5. Closing the sale	5. Regression testing	5. Negotiating T's & C's	5. Pulling orders	5. Tracking bugs	5. Calibrating test equipment	5. Managing service lifecycle	5. Setting behavioral expectations	5. Managing capital sources	5. Managing fundamentals
6. Influencing industry opinion leaders	6. Contracting	6. Validating produce-ability	6. Signing the agreements	6. Building product	6. Administering new releases to existing customers	6. Filing compliance documents	6. Delivering IT applications	6. Monitoring performance	6. Managing accounts payable	6. Ensuring effective corrective action
7. Pricing	7. Cross selling	7. Releasing to production	7. Facilitating the connections with product development	7. Producing product	7. Tracking customer release data	7. Ensuring key controls are maintained	7. Managing IT projects	7. Compensating performance	7. Managing accounts receivable	7. Monitoring breakthroughs
8. Promoting company & products	8. Managing accounts	8. Identifying & protecting intellectual property	8. Managing the relationship	8. Integrating hardware & software			8. Managing suppliers	8. Managing benefits	8. Financial reporting	
9. Developing leads	9. Managing key relationships	9. Managing product end-of-life	9. Renewing/discontinuing alliances that no longer fit	9. Validating product quality			9. Developing staff & Leadership	9. Rewarding performance	9. Managing investor relationships	
				10. Shipping			10. Minimizing risk	10. Recognizing contributions	10. Ensuring SEC compliance	
							11. Managing performance	11. Reviewing performance		

90

Figure 5.6 NOW Fundamentals Map for BearPaw

	OPERATING PROCESSES						SUPPORTING				
	Assessing & Accessing Markets	Selling	Developing Products	Managing Strategic Alliances	Producing Products	Servicing Products	Ensuring Compliance	Utilizing Information	Attracting & Developing Team Members	Managing Finances	Managing Business Performance
PROCESS MEASURES	• # of new product ideas/ enhancements approved for development • # of column inches of coverage in targeted trade pubs • # leads generated • % leads that convert to prospects	• # prospects in the funnel • # of qualified leads • # of proposals presented • Win/loss ratio on proposals • Average deal $'s • $ from cross selling	• Project performance to initial specifications • Project deliver to original target date • Project cost versus original plan • Actual cost to produce vs. estimated cost to produce	• # of active strategic alliances • % alliances rating us as a partner at 8 or better • Alliance partners on-time performance	• % out-of-box failure rate • Actual material costs vs. standard cost • Actual labor cost vs. standard cost • Actual production output vs. scheduled • Shipping date vs. original commitment date	• % calls with first-call resolution • % customer calls escalated to engineering • # of known, active bugs • Time to resolve known bugs	• ISO level of certification • % key controls validates • % of key controls current • On-time calibration to plan • On-time compliance document filing	• % IT budget to revenue • % external customer satisfied • % uptime • % high value projects on time • % IT staff turnover • % business continuity plan current • Information security risk rating	• # days to fill open position • Employee satisfaction with compensation • Employee satisfaction with benefits • % on-time completion of team member performance	• Performance to budget • Cash to plan • Average days aging on receivables • Average days aging on payables • # days to close after quarter end	• % outcome measures in corrective action • % process measures in corrective action • % breakthrough strategies in green • Quarterly reviews conducted on time
PROCESS OWNER	Coralie Hayes	Ed Israel	Matt Hixson	Kelly Ferguson	Manny Garcia	Raj Rajahasan	Brent Shaw	Mike Green	Brian Powers	Sarah Fridley	Casey Hayes
OUTCOME MEASURES	Revenue	Total Return To Shareholders	ED/TDA	Cash On Hand	Ideas Implemented Per Employee	Customer Retention	Customer Referrals	New Product Revenue	Volunteer Hours	Dollars Contributed to Non-Profits / Turnover	Engaged Workforce

NOW Management System

91

Mapping the Fundamentals

Over the past 20 years the NOW Fundamentals Map, which evolved from our work with Baker Boyer Bank's leaders, has benefited nearly 100 diverse organizations, including a high school, a university-level nursing school, a high-end customer window-covering manufacturer, a large financial services business, several medical equipment and device companies, wood products companies, a global supply chain company, multiple software and technology companies, a family restaurant and pub, the executive branch of a state government, a corrections system, and a Christian missionary organization.

Figure 5.6 offers a high-level view of a NOW Fundamentals Map for our fictional company BearPaw, introduced in Chapter 2.

Laying the Foundation

As a leader, you must define the mission of your organization. The mission is not mere words, however compellingly etched in granite over the entrance to corporate headquarters. It's a foundational piece of a system that creates the living and breathing context for all people to do their work.

You must create a compelling context for the work that will follow, and establish the need for a highly organized and energized system to fulfill the vision.

Whichever approach you use, your management system needs to address five foundational elements, as charted in Figure 5.7:

- ◆ What business are you in (Mission)?
- ◆ What beliefs will guide your actions (Values)?
- ◆ What do you want your business to be known for (Vision)?
- ◆ What accomplishments will define your success (Key Goals)?
- ◆ What will gauge progress toward your goals (Outcome Measures)?

Most organizations do address these foundational elements, but many fail to take the next crucial step that will move them from the abstract leadership level to the concrete, operational management

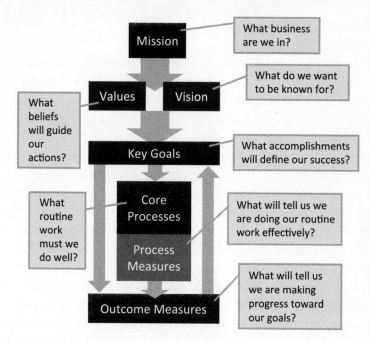

FIGURE 5.7 Foundational Elements of a Management System

level. Leadership may know *where* it wants the organization to go, but management needs to know *how* to take it there.

Two additional elements close the gap between *where* and *how*:

- ◆ What routine work must you do well (Core Processes)?
- ◆ What will show that you are doing the routine work well (Process Measures)?

The individuals who do the work that helps us achieve our goals rarely see the direct connection between what they do and the organization's larger goals. Traditional departments fail to make those connections, for a variety of reasons, but primarily because the critical work of organizations rarely takes place within a single functional area; instead, it moves across multiple areas. Most work is cross-functional and occurs through a set of interdependent processes that collectively produce and support products and services. For your employees to appreciate the context for acting in the now, they need to see how the process within which they work connects to the organization's goals.

That's why defining core processes is so vitally important. Only then can you clearly see *how* the work actually gets done. When leaders create a shared language for talking about the business, they propel everyone to concentrate on how work actually gets done and how they might improve it.

To operate at the speed of now demands a systematic/intentional design that eliminates the confusion and drama so often generated by seat-of-the-pants/unconscious differing views of how to run the business. The shift from opinion-and-emotion-driven mentality to fact-based thinking neutralizes the frustration that drives most internal management conflict. It levels the playing field, as the persuasive extroverts no longer win resources on the sheer power of their personalities. With all the facts on the table, common sense prevails and a deep sense of teamwork emerges. And, most importantly, sharpened clarity enables all employees to climb aboard, each doing her part.

When you think of management as a system, as a collection of core processes, then you can begin to organize the work everyone must do in order to achieve your organization's goals (see Figure 5.8). That work should consume the vast majority of the resources in most businesses. While most businesses organize themselves along functional lines (such as marketing, sales, engineering, quality, customer service, accounting and finance, and human resources), an organization's work processes cross back and forth between functional departments. Four steps will help you get a firm grip on your core processes:

Step 1: Identify core processes. What routine work must your organization do well in order to attain the outcome measures that prove you are achieving your key goals?

Step 2: Define subprocesses. What routine activities must collectively work well in order for the core processes to deliver on expectations?

Step 3: Create process measures. What measures will tell us that this process is meeting our expectations? Mass Ingenuity's clients use

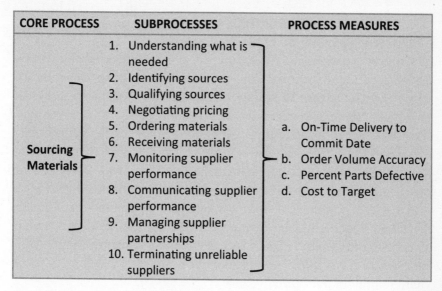

CORE PROCESS	SUBPROCESSES	PROCESS MEASURES
Sourcing Materials	1. Understanding what is needed 2. Identifying sources 3. Qualifying sources 4. Negotiating pricing 5. Ordering materials 6. Receiving materials 7. Monitoring supplier performance 8. Communicating supplier performance 9. Managing supplier partnerships 10. Terminating unreliable suppliers	a. On-Time Delivery to Commit Date b. Order Volume Accuracy c. Percent Parts Defective d. Cost to Target

FIGURE **5.8** Management as System

red/yellow/green scorecards to make it easy to grasp the status of process measures. However you decide to do it, make sure people can easily see and understand the scores.

Step 4: Assign an owner. Every core process needs to be clearly owned by one individual who serves as the primary advocate for this process, monitors its performance, and drives any needed corrective action.

In the process of identifying all of your core processes, subprocesses, and process measures you will discover what makes your business tick by answering some important questions:

- ◆ Who takes accountability for the cross-functional processes that drive our business?
- ◆ What are the constraints that currently restrain our success?
- ◆ Have we allocated our resources appropriately?
- ◆ How do we identify problems?
- ◆ How do we connect each and every employee to our goals?

Connecting Every Employee

When "Jeb Jacobs," head of purchasing for "Global Corp," discovered that the company's new Gulfstream business jet contained parts "Made in Mexico," he did not bat an eye. Jeb had done his homework and knew that Gulfstream Mexicali's 335,000-square-foot, 1,100-employee manufacturing facility had won the 2010 Shingo Prize for operational excellence (named after Shigeo Shingo, the man largely credited with the design of the Toyota Just-in-Time production system, the precursor to Lean.) This accomplishment meant that Mexicali's electrical wire harnesses, sheet-metal details, assemblies, and machined parts surpassed industry standards. Gulfstream, a division of General Dynamics, won the prize because of performance improvements that occurred while the company implemented nearly 34,000 ideas that actually saved the organization $1.3 million in 2008, and more than $7 million over three years.

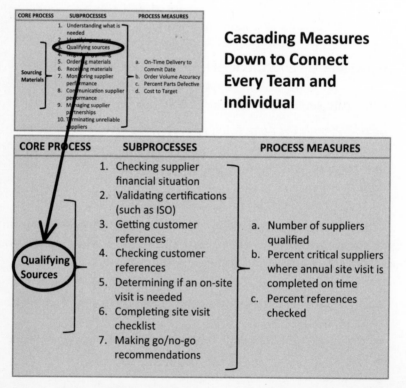

Cascading Measures Down to Connect Every Team and Individual

FIGURE 5.9   Breaking Down Processes

How did that happen? Gulfstream Mexicali's leadership connected every employee to the business by giving each of them an explicit role in the improvement effort. That involved making the goals of the business crystal clear and creating a context that inspired innovation.

Another means of connection involves breaking down the sub-processes within your core processes to the next level (see Figure 5.9). This exercise of breaking down the processes can continue until you connect every single employee to the process they manage, whether as an individual or as part of a team.

In our consulting practice we create what we call a line-of-sight system, making it crystal clear to each employee how her work connects to the core processes and, ultimately, to the business outcome measures. The NOW Fundamentals Map offers a handy tool for doing that. Ken Schiller and Brian Nolen, owners of Rudy's Country Store & Bar-B-Q and Mighty Fine Burgers, Fries and Shakes, had found another model for doing this in the Baldrige framework. Individual scorecards work like their organizational cousins, using red/yellow/green ranges of performance to drive individual focus and action. Individual performance that falls into the red or yellow range demands corrective action with Mass Ingenuity's Seven-Step Problem-Solving methodology, which will be explained in Chapter 8. This technique sounds the death knell for the dreaded annual performance appraisal, replacing it with dynamic real-time feedback in the now. The old approach led to waste, disconnection, misconnection, and confusion. The new one forges the connection and clarity that keeps an organization growing and advancing.

■ ■ ■

Complete the Speedometer for the Working in the NOW Business (Table 5.1) and add your net score to the summary sheet in the Appendix.

TABLE 5.1 NOW Speedometer 5: Working in the NOW Business

Then	−1	0	+1	Now
We make decisions based on opinions and influence				We base decisions on facts
We believe that the boss is the most important customer				We believe that whoever receives our work is our customer
We focus on doing the work and rarely try to improve how it gets done				We see work as a process and continuously strive to improve how work gets done
We see performance measures as a private matter between boss and employee				We keep measures out in the open for everyone to see
We just do whatever our boss tells us to do				We do what our scorecards measure
We don't understand the goals nor our part in them				We make sure everyone understands the goals and their role in achieving them
We see the annual performance review as the primary source of employee feedback				We get near real-time feedback through individual scorecards
Subtotals				
Working in the Now NET SCORE				

Add this score to the consolidated score in the Appendix.

THEN   NOW

−7 −6 −5 −4 −3 −2 −1 |0| +1 +2 +3 +4 +5 +6 +7

Working on the NOW Business

Achieve Critical Breakthroughs

I n late 1999, Steve Berglas, writing in *Inc.* magazine, offered a scathing observation of Apple's founder: "[Steve] Jobs, like virtually all charismatic leaders, also has a well-documented dark side that causes him to mutate from mesmerizing allure to sadistic perfectionism, often without discernible provocation. Apple's current board of directors, although they did well to exploit Jobs's charms . . . must now pull the plug before his arrogant and demeaning interpersonal style undoes all the good he has done."

Time, of course, has proven Berglas wrong. Jobs went on to engineer one of the most spectacular corporate turnarounds in modern business history.

Seven years later, in a CNN interview, Daniel Morgan of Synovus Investment Advisors joked, "Apple had plastic surgery and liposuction and a boob job." Apple, actually, underwent more than a cosmetic transformation. Apple created one breakthrough product after another on its way to establishing itself as the ultimate cool brand.

Apple's sustained success does not depend solely on its unique and charismatic leader. It relies even more on skilled and purposeful planning and execution of initiatives at every level of the organization. As Tim Cook, now Apple's chief executive officer, said in January 2011, when Steve Jobs took a second medical leave from the company,

"In my view, Apple is doing its best work ever. The team here has an unparalleled breadth and depth of talent and a culture of innovation. . . . Excellence has become a habit." Those words describe a NOW organization, one that makes excellence through breakthroughs a habit.

Warning! You don't create a NOW organization with magic or prayers or a celebrity leader. You do it the old-fashioned way, with a lot of mind-bending, backbreaking effort. What makes the difference between good companies and great companies? The ability to deliver breakthroughs. The world's most brilliant idea and marketing strategy will go nowhere without flawless execution. The faster the execution, the faster a company will race ahead of its competitors.

In this chapter we explore two ways to achieve breakthroughs in execution: improving the performance of existing processes, and developing new capabilities. These kinds of breakthroughs must happen at all levels of the organization, from the office of the CEO to every desk in customer service.

The Source of Breakthroughs

Consider the iPad: "One million iPads in 28 days—that's less than half of the 74 days it took to achieve this milestone with iPhone," Jobs exclaimed. It happened because the product is deeply cool. It happened because the product was skillfully marketed. But behind the product and the packaging and the buzz, you'll find a huge amount of hard-grinding and disciplined work. Jobs may have supplied the inspiration, but everyone in the company, top to bottom, strives for excellence. A breakthrough may spring from a single brilliant insight by a genius like Steve Jobs, but the vast majority of breakthroughs result from careful planning and exquisite execution.

Breakthroughs fall into one of two basic categories, as shown in Table 6.1 and further defined here.

◆ *A performance breakthrough is a step-function improvement in an existing work process.* These improvements are not small, incremental changes; rather, they are the result of considerably hard, organized, and complex work. It is easy to see how a

TABLE **6.1** Breakthrough Categories

Breakthrough Type	Definition	Example
Performance	The step-function improvement in the performance of an existing process	Reducing the time it takes to resolve a customer problem by 30 percent
Capability	Development of a new process	Replacing in-house software development with external offshore software development

rapidly growing company like Apple would need to have these kinds of breakthroughs occurring routinely. Some drivers of performance breakthroughs include:

- Growth demands a level of output you cannot currently produce.
- Market circumstances force you to lower your product costs.
- Customers expect a level of quality your company cannot currently achieve.
- Competitors have increased their market share because they respond more quickly to orders.
- Materials cost fluctuations challenge you to forecast profitability accurately.
- Rework costs have eaten into your profits.
- Customer service calls, too long and unproductive, cause customers to hang up.
- Performance reports arrive late and hamper management decision making.
- Product development team runs behind schedule 90 percent of the time.

◆ *A capability breakthrough creates brand new competencies.* Many companies made a classic capability breakthrough when they added online retailing to their brick-and mortar tradition.

If the word "breakthrough" conjures up the image of a mad scientist shouting "Eureka!" think again. The true picture resembles a well-designed architectural blueprint. You don't wait for miracles to happen, you *plan* for them to happen and then you *make* them happen. "Chance favors the prepared mind," noted

Louis Pasteur. A variety of reasons may drive the need for capability breakthroughs:

- Strategic plans require moving a previously outsourced process in-house.
- Competitors have added a new service you must duplicate.
- Circumstances force you to switch from direct sales to value-added resellers.
- Public offerings demand a whole new level of financial controls.
- Customer service efficiency requires a shift from local offices to a central call center.
- Spreadsheets are no longer sufficient to run your business.
- Acquisition strategy creates a need for a way to identify, acquire, and integrate targets.

Whatever their origins, breakthrough initiatives don't succeed unless they are skillfully executed. In a world where speed rules, you can no longer rely on the old annual planning scenario to keep up with and surpass your competitors. If a company enthusiastically launches a dozen initiatives, it is likely that only four of those will be successfully implemented, four will fail, and the rest will need more time to be executed. More initiatives would be successful if the members of the organization developed the skill to plan and the skills to execute at every level in the organization. Bear in mind that this is not about an organization's strategic planning, but about the operational planning needed to *execute* its strategy.

Many leaders and managers feel frustrated when strategic planning fails to affect day-to-day operations. All too often executives create marvelous strategic plans but later wonder why they were never implemented. To achieve strategic plans, especially ambitious ones, you must not only plan for requisite breakthroughs, you must make them operational, as illustrated in Figure 6.1.

The strategic direction of the organization establishes the context for breakthroughs. Once you set the right strategic direction, you must assess current performance and capability in an effort to determine whether or not they are sufficient to support the strategy. If not, you must plan the breakthroughs that will close the gap between strategy and your organization's ability to achieve it.

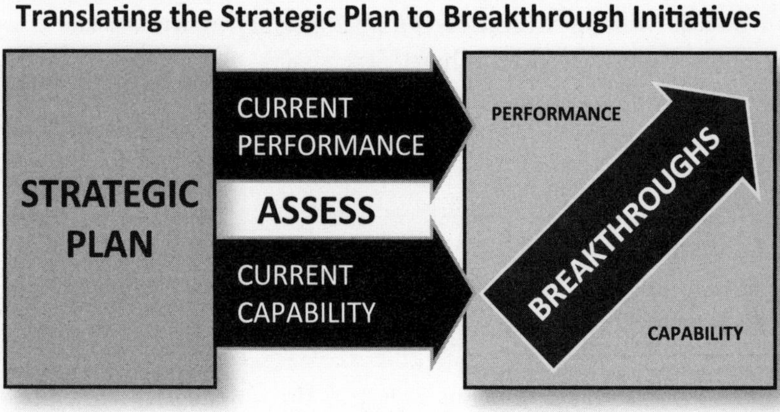

Translating the Strategic Plan to Breakthrough Initiatives

FIGURE **6.1** Executing a Strategic Plan

Creating the Skill to Plan at All Levels

"We spent nearly a day of our last two-day off-site retreat arguing over *words*," complained the COO of a fast-growing software start-up. "Everyone got frustrated because we all come from different companies and we all plan differently. We even argued for more than an hour over what 'strategy' means, and never came to an agreement."

Effective planning requires that all involved share a common language, which includes a set of agreed-upon words, terms, logic, and formats. Organizations that lack a shared vocabulary for planning invariably end up with plans from various teams that bear little resemblance to one another. In order to add discipline to the planning process and ensure that everyone can easily read and comprehend every plan, you want to pick one planning method and make it the standard up and down the organization. To make it easy for individuals to master and use it, remember to KISS (keep it simple, stupid). In the NOW Management System, we use a planning method that consists of three templates anyone can use to create and manage breakthroughs at any level of an organization.

Whatever planning tool you use, it should provide a common language everyone can learn to speak. You may recall one of the Seven Deadly Sins of Management, listed in Chapter 2: "Inconsistent Language." Without a consistent vocabulary for discussing planning, your people will waste a lot of valuable time trying to translate what they are trying to tell each other.

Before you start the planning meeting, you might review your vocabulary, or even distribute a printed glossary. Your own planning toolset should:

1. Communicate the plan.
2. Organize the work.
3. Ensure execution.

The first tool our team uses is the Breakthrough Plan, which incorporates five elements on a single page, shown in Figure 6.2:

- *Objective*: What we will accomplish
- *Target*: How we will measure our success
- *Situation*: The problems we must solve and the opportunities we plan to seize
- *Strategies*: How we plan to solve the problems and seize the opportunities
- *Subtargets*: How we will measure the success of our strategies

BREAKTHROUGH PLAN

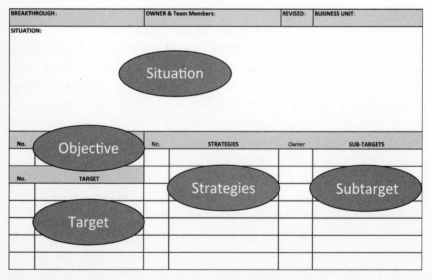

FIGURE 6.2 Five Elements of a Breakthrough Plan

BREAKTHOUGH WORKPLAN

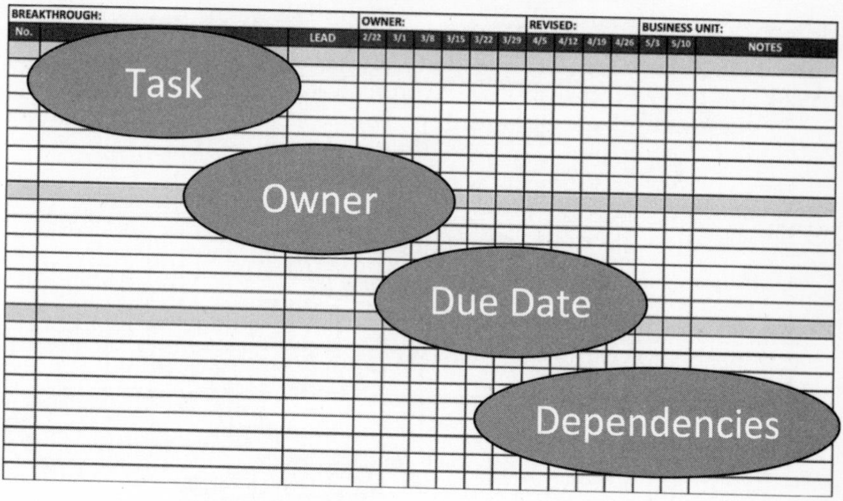

FIGURE **6.3** Breakthrough Workplan

Once we have developed the Breakthrough Plan, we translate it into the next tool, a Breakthrough Workplan, that displays the details that will organize, drive, and coordinate execution (see Figure 6.3). The workplan defines the tasks required to implement each strategy, assigns ownership for each task, sets a schedule or due dates for completion, and describes other variables and dependencies that may affect successful completion of the task.

The vocabulary of the Breakthrough Workplan promotes understanding and facilitates alignment among all stakeholders. It also serves as a valuable way to check if those doing the work are moving in the right direction.

Once everyone understands the details in the workplan, the real work begins. To measure progress, you need a tool to assess how far you have come and how far you need to go to make the breakthrough a reality. In our toolset, we conduct a Breakthrough Status Review to assess each strategy and formally mark progress toward the breakthrough relative to the plan (see Figure 6.4). The review reveals which, if any, of the Breakthrough Plan's elements need adjustment or rethinking. Owners of each strategy in the Breakthrough Plan report progress, concerns about the plan's eventual success, and actions they are taking to get an errant plan back on track.

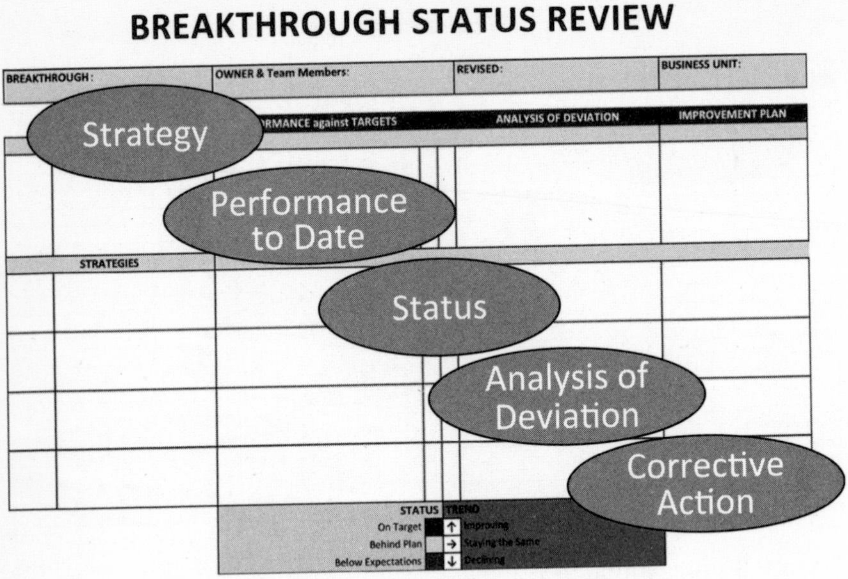

BREAKTHROUGH STATUS REVIEW

FIGURE 6.4 Breakthrough Status Review

Using tools such as these help to create a shared language that everyone understands. And, understanding fuels speed. To get your organization moving at the speed of now, you need a powerful, common toolset for planning and executing breakthroughs.

Performance Breakthroughs in Action

Three weeks into a performance breakthrough project, "Jacque Sevrain," a furnace tender at "Woodlands Products" in Rutherglen, Ontario, Canada, noted something odd on the plant manager's weekly report. "The number 17 caught my eye," he said. "Before I came over to my new job, I operated a machine in the mill that recorded pressure during the plywood manufacturing process, and 17 was the set point for the machine. I went through earlier reports and could not understand why that number was on *every* report for the past year and a half."

Sevrain had plucked that one number out of a multipage computer-generated report the plant manager received every week. Knowing that the quantity of top-grade plywood coming out of the mill had been running below normal for a year and a half, Sevrain wondered if that might somehow relate to the recurring 17 over the same period. When Sevrain and another member of the Performance Breakthrough Team talked to "Jimmie Davis," the new recruit responsible for running the machine, they made an interesting discovery.

Davis told them, "The person who had this job before me told me to write down 17 on the clipboard at the end of every shift, or I would get in trouble." Sure enough, the record sheet clipboard dangling from a screw near the large pressure gauge on the side of the machine showed an endless series of 17s. Davis demonstrated how he could turn the dial on the gauge from 13 to 17 with a flick of his wrist.

Servain chuckled. "Did anyone ever tell you that during the shift you were supposed to keep adjusting that dial, trying to keep the needle on 17, and then at the end of the shift you were supposed to record the gauge's reading *before* you adjusted it back to 17?"

"No," confessed Davis.

As it turned out, that discovery and a handful of other small improvements that emerged during the three-and-a-half-month project added nearly $3 million dollars to the plant's annual bottom line.

When you embark on a performance breakthrough, you'll usually see a few specific adjustments you can make. However, you should prepare for a surprise or two. Facts reveal truth, and the truth can take you by surprise. While understandable in hindsight, Davis's mistake really surprised Servain. Fixing it not only corrected the problem, it also placed accountability where it belonged: with the person doing the work. Going forward, Davis will record true measurements, and his accurate counting will help him take accountability for his work.

Performance breakthroughs like the one the Woodlands Products team accomplished require an effective methodology. That methodology, like the Breakthrough Planning toolset described earlier, becomes a part of an organization's language.

Over the years, various methodologies for performance breakthroughs have emerged from the quality movement, among them these three process improvement methods:

- ◆ Kaizen
- ◆ Lean
- ◆ Six Sigma

You have probably heard of, and may have even used, the others, but to refresh your memory, the Japanese word *kaizen* means "improvement" or "change for the better." It encompasses a philosophy and practice of continuous improvement and has been broadly applied across all industries. Kaizen "events" occur in concentrated 3- to 5-day intense performance improvement efforts during which people attack a given problem aggressively, swiftly identifying and launching solutions. If you want to learn more about this proven methodology, take a look at *How to Do Kaizen: A New Path to Innovation* by Norman Bodek and Bunji Tozawa, or *The Kaizen Blitz: Accelerating Breakthroughs in Productivity and Performance* by Anthony C. Laraia, Patricia E. Moody, and Robert W. Hall.

Lean traces its origins to the Toyota (Just-in-Time) Production System. This methodology defines as waste any expenditure of resources that does not directly add value the customer will purchase. It aims to eliminate all forms of waste from storage to movement to waiting to overprocessing. While it began as a manufacturing philosophy, today companies apply it to any and all areas of an organization. The body of work in Lean is increasingly specialized with materials and classes available in many specialties. An example is *Lean IT: Enabling and Sustaining Your Lean Transformation* by Steven Bell and Michael Orzen.

Six Sigma, developed by Motorola in 1986, focuses on identifying and removing the errors that cause defects, as well as minimizing variability in manufacturing and business processes. It utilizes a set of tools and methods guided by specially trained people within the organization (known as Six Sigma Black Belts) who follow a defined sequence of steps with a quantified financial target to reduce costs. A process that achieves Six Sigma status will turn out only 3.4 defects per million parts produced. For more about this methodology, consult *Six Sigma: The Breakthrough Strategy Revolutionizing the World's Top Corporations* by Mikel Harry and Richard Schroeder.

Although it doesn't matter which tool you use, you should bear in mind that a powerful methodology such as Six Sigma, with its emphasis on specialists in the methodology, can result in an organization with two classes of workers: those who "get it" and those who don't. In a NOW organization, *everyone* must grow adept at solving problems, not just a band of specialists. That argues for a basic problem-solving and process improvement approach everyone can learn to use. We'll delve more deeply into this subject in Chapter 8, with special emphasis on a Seven-Step Problem-Solving methodology.

Breakthroughs in Capability

How do you start doing something you've never done before? Boston Police Department (BPD) Superintendent John Daly set about doing just that when he decided to incorporate Twitter into BPD's 911 emergency call center. As he explained in a press conference, "I would like to have someone just sitting at a position in with the dispatchers, kind of cognizant of everything that's going on in the city, just sending out tweets in real time for things that will affect people."

He knew, however, that doing something brand new might pose some dangers. "So the other thing we are going to do with Twitter—and we have to be very careful because there is a kind of Big Brother aspect to this—but using the Twitter advance search we can look at all the tweets in Boston in real time. . . . When people start saying, 'What's that smoke coming from the Hancock Tower,' or 'Why is everyone running around Copley Place,' . . . we can ask, 'Is something going on?'" While Daly envisioned Twitter as an effective early-warning system, he realized his people had to experiment with it before it became a new capability.

Every organization comes to a point when it must develop a new capability or risk losing its competitiveness. Dynamic organizations that function effectively in the now constantly pursue new capabilities needed to meet the speed of the customer's need. A new capability adds a new competence that an organization can deploy to accommodate shifts in the market, customer behavior and preferences, technology, the competitive environment, the global arena, and any other changes that force it to alter its business goals or strategies.

New capabilities include such new competencies as implementing a NOW Management System, deploying a social media strategy, transitioning to cloud computing, and adapting to the millennial mind-set.

To paraphrase psychiatrist R. D. Laing, "We conduct business in such a speeded-up world that we can only see the present in our

TABLE **6.2** Seven Phases of Creating New Capabilities

Creating New Capability		
Phase I	Define	*Define the business problem or opportunity and the scope of the project.*
Phase II	Analyze	*Analyze the current situation and develop possibilities for the future state.*
Phase III	Design	*Design the desired future state in detail.*
Phase IV	Build	*Build out the detailed workplans to get to the future state.*
Phase V	Implement	*Implement the workplans and the future state.*
Phase VI	Evaluate	*Evaluate the project and the performance of the new process.*
Phase VII	Sustain	*Sustain the new capability, moving it to the disciplines, routines, and controls of a core process.*

rearview mirror." Since operating successfully in such a rapidly changing world requires the ability to master new capabilities, every organization needs a well-designed, systematic way to pinpoint and develop those capabilities. It takes so much time and energy and money to incorporate new skills and methodologies, you want to do it efficiently. Otherwise, they may do more harm than good.

Unlike performance improvement, the methodologies to develop new capabilities are hard to find. But, like performance improvement, developing a language and process for this kind of breakthrough is essential.

The most effective capability breakthroughs progress through seven phases, delineated in Table 6.2 and defined in greater detail here.

Phase I: Define

This phase establishes the project's charter and produces a shared understanding by all involved. By defining the business problem or opportunity and the scope of the project, you set clear expectations from the outset. Your definition should specify the project's sponsor, leader, participants, and resources.

To determine whether or not you can move from one phase to the next, you conduct a Phase Gate Review, whereby the team presents a standardized checklist of all the work the team needs to have completed at the current stage before the project's sponsors can approve transition to the next phase. This rigor dramatically improves the odds of successful capability breakthrough efforts.

Let's imagine how the Boston Police Department (BPD) might have employed the seven phases in its effort to incorporate Twitter into its emergency call system.

Having decided that Twitter offers an opportunity for the BPD, Superintendent Daly describes the scope of the plan in his press conference when he talks about appointing someone to send out tweets from the 911 emergency call center about events occurring in the city. He also describes how monitoring tweets could provide the BPD with early warnings about potential problems, but also makes it clear he is worried about possible misuses of the medium.

PHASE II: ANALYZE

In this phase, the project team validates and expands the charter by more thoroughly detailing the project, its scope, and the resources required for success. The project team gathers extensive data inside the organization, and even outside the organization, in an effort to understand the knowledge and expertise the organization will need to implement the initiative successfully. They seek information on "best practices" and begin to specify the desired future state. The Analyze Phase also includes tentative work role definitions, training needs, change and risk management factors, and ways to measure performance. Again, a rigorous Phase Gate Review will determine whether the breakthrough project team is ready to progress to the next phase.

The BPD team assigned to the Twitter project will analyze how best to use this new tool by looking at what others are doing, and by gaining insight into what works and what doesn't in the land of tweets. They'll then begin to define how they envision Twitter working for the department in the future. That vision will include defining roles, specifying training, and recommending risk management protocols and performance measures for monitoring effectiveness.

PHASE III: DESIGN

Once the team has finished its analysis and gotten approval to proceed, they tackle the Design Phase. This includes a detailed workplan with tasks and deliverables. The plan will include such items as a map of future state processes, recommended measures and controls, role descriptions, training programs, and resource and technology acquisition. Once again, moving from Phase III to Phase IV requires the successful completion of a detailed Phase Gate Review.

In the case of BPD's Twitter opportunity, the detailed design comes together as the team maps out exactly how the work will flow in the future, who will do what, what staffing the project requires, how to hire and train new talent, when to acquire necessary technology, and which performance measures the organization will use to measure progress. Their detailed step-by-step workplan, or project plan, shows exactly how to implement the initiative.

PHASE IV: BUILD

Once a Phase Gate Review permits the team to move to the Build Phase, the team can actually set about getting everything in place to implement the initiative, including processes and procedures documentation, job descriptions, performance measure scorecards (including red/yellow/green ranges), training materials, acquisition of needed resources, risk management techniques, and detailed plans to close all gaps and complete all tasks needed to implement the new capability. The Phase Gate Review leads to go/no-go decision.

The Boston Police Department would now finalize the designs created during Phase IV.

PHASE V: IMPLEMENT

With everything in place, the time has arrived to *do* it. During the Implement Phase, the organization rolls out the new process, recruiting and training people for the new roles, putting the technology to work, and executing the new capability. If the team has done its earlier work well, change will occur smoothly and with few surprises. When surprises do pop up (and they always do), people use predetermined risk management protocols to deal with them, quickly and effectively. The established performance measures constantly gauge progress. The Phase Gate Review for Phase V validates that that the new capability has transitioned into a routine process.

BPD Twitter has gone live. Scorecards for monitoring performance follow the red-yellow-green logic as the Twitter program transitions from initial implementation to a new fundamental for BPD. When problems occur, the department addresses them immediately.

PHASE VI: EVALUATE

In this phase, the organization will evaluate the project to see if the performance level fulfills the original expectations. If not, the organization makes necessary adjustments to get the new capability functioning at the level required to support the goals and strategies of the breakthrough. When the applause dies down, the organization can turn its attention to its next big breakthrough, be it a brand-new capability or enhancement of the new one's performance.

During the Evaluate Phase, Superintendent Daly would sit down with his BPD's breakthrough project team and debrief them. He might ask, "Is Twitter meeting our expectations? Are we seeing any unexpected problems? Can we make it better?" If it turns out that the new capability has met or surpassed expectations, everyone deserves a pat on the back. One enterprising young officer might wonder aloud, "Has anyone been playing with Apple's new iPad? I think it might make an amazing addition to our community policing efforts."

PHASE VII: SUSTAIN

Finally, the new capability transitions into the Sustain Phase, where it functions as a routine process in the business, or a *fundamental.* As a new fundamental, it will now merit continuous monitoring; and, eventually, it might well require a performance breakthrough to maximize its contribution.

With luck, BPD's Superintendent Daly will succeed in using Twitter to improve the safety in his city. Over time, the department would surely tweak and perfect it, even if they add a new capability with the iPad.

Sequencing, Coordinating, and Seeing

> *"Would you tell me, please, which way I ought to go from here?"* asked Alice.
>
> *"That depends a good deal on where you want to get to,"* said the Cat.
>
> *"I don't much care where,"* said Alice.
>
> *"Then it doesn't matter which way you go,"* said the Cat.

"—so long as I get somewhere," Alice added as an explanation.

"Oh, you're sure to do that," said the Cat, "if you only walk long enough."

—Lewis Carroll, *Through the Looking Glass,*
and What Alice Found There (1871)

If you don't know where you're going, you're sure to get there. Breakthroughs do not merely fall like rain on an organization, they happen because the organization planned for them to happen. Effective leaders know exactly where they want their organizations to go, and demand clear paths for getting there. No matter how large or complex or unimaginable the change you want to make, only smart planning will assure your success.

As leaders think about the performance and capability breakthroughs, they need to make sure they effectively sequence, coordinate, and communicate them to everyone. Proper sequencing matters when initiatives depend on each other.

To further its goal to reduce costs, "Rocks 'R' Us" may plan to shift order processing to an online system in order to cut the time it takes for its customer service reps to process orders for its commercial clients. Suppose, however, that the company has also embarked on a plan to completely overhaul its website. The new order processing system will depend on completing the work on the updated website. Surprisingly, many companies will launch both initiatives simultaneously, and end up with little to show for their efforts but conflict and confusion.

Leaders often find it hard to communicate complicated long-term strategic plans in a way that everyone can easily grasp, yet successful implementation always depends on clear communication. To bridge that gap, we have developed the NOW Breakthrough Map to display a satellite view of long-range breakthrough plans (see Figure 6.5). Each box in the outer ring represents one of this year's breakthroughs, while the boxes in the two inner rings show planned breakthroughs for the next two years.

In most cases, an organization should restrict its strategic breakthrough initiatives to two to three per year. Strategic breakthroughs, the major, organizationwide initiatives that consume significant resources, will play a major role in achieving the organization's goals.

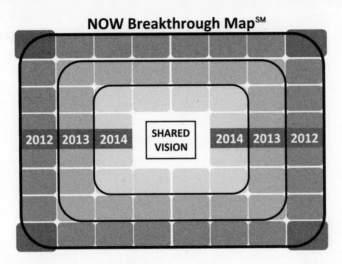

FIGURE 6.5 NOW Breakthrough Map

The NOW Breakthrough Map also depicts the tactical breakthroughs that demand far fewer resources and involve a narrower part of the organization.

Take a look at BearPaw's NOW Breakthrough Map in Figure 6.6. Don't let its complexity throw you. It looks a little busy because it consolidates everything into a snapshot of the company's initiatives. Behind each box for the current year sits a written Breakthrough Plan, with three designated as the large Strategic Breakthroughs (S1, S2, and S3), and the balance designated as smaller Tactical Breakthroughs (T1, T2, T3, etc.). BearPaw posts this map and its NOW Fundamentals Map throughout the company to facilitate understanding of what the company expects to accomplish in the future.

Initiatives in the inner rings may depend on successful completion of ones in the outer ring.

The best-laid plans can go awry, but badly laid plans pave the path to corporate hell. Or, to paraphrase Vince Lombardi, "Planning isn't everything, but no planning isn't anything."

For a business to succeed in our superfast world, it must constantly make breakthroughs in both performance and capability. These initiatives create a multitude of NOW Moments, moments when people need to make good decisions quickly. The skills, knowledge, and authority you give your workforce to make those decisions will

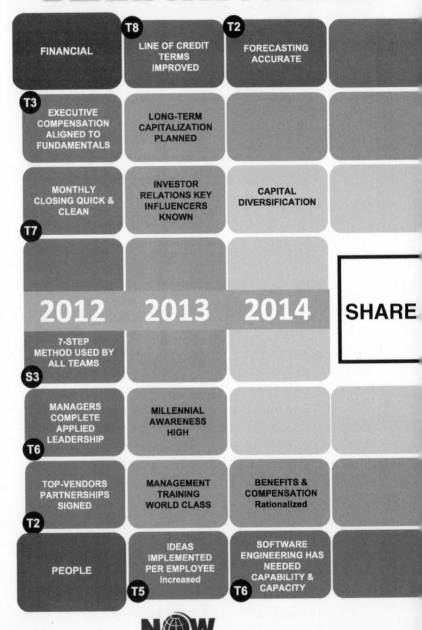

FIGURE 6.6   NOW Breakthrough Map for BearPaw

NOW BREAKTHROUGH MAP^{SM}

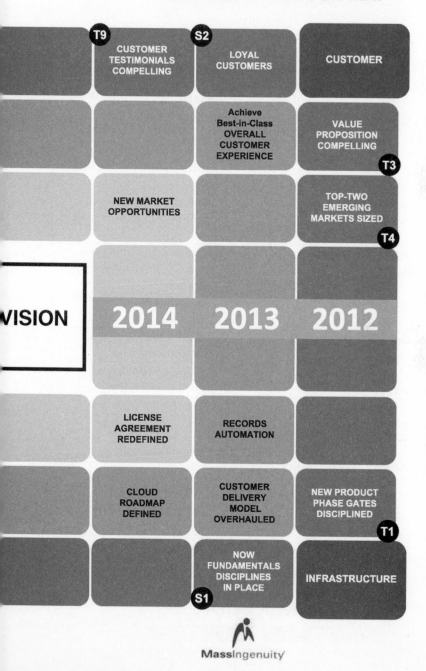

determine whether or not your organization can effectively function in the now.

• • •

Complete the Speedometer for Working on the NOW Business (Table 6.3) and add your net score to the summary sheet in the Appendix.

TABLE 6.3　NOW Speedometer 6: Working on the NOW Business

Then	−1	0	+1	Now
We don't understand what a breakthrough really is				We skillfully and routinely execute breakthrough initiatives
We have created no real track record of success in achieving major improvements in our routine work				When we set out to achieve a significant improvement in performance, we expect success
We do a poor job of developing new capabilities				If we need to develop a new capability, we know how to do it effectively
We lack strong planning skills				We all know how to plan effectively
We do not use a systematic planning process				We use a common language and method for planning
We cannot all cite this year's major initiatives				We all understand the major initiatives for the year
We do not carefully monitor progress on initiatives				We carefully monitor the progress of all initiatives
Subtotals				

Working on the Now **NET SCORE** ☐

Add this score to the consolidated score in the Appendix.

SPEEDOMETER

THEN		NOW
-7 -6 -5 -4 -3 -2 -1	0	+1 +2 +3 +4 +5 +6 +7

7

Creating NOW Transparency

Close the Execution Gap

On September 15, 2008, just five days after too-big-to-fail Lehman Brothers had filed for Chapter 11 in Manhattan Bankruptcy Court, Judge James Peck ruled, "I must approve this transaction because it is the only available transaction. This is the most momentous bankruptcy hearing I've ever sat through. It can never be deemed precedent for future cases. It's hard for me to imagine a similar emergency."

Little did Judge Peck realize he was seeing the beginning of the Great Recession, one that would sink hundreds of major corporations, including the once most powerful corporation in the world, General Motors.

Why had no one seen it coming? Because this disaster, shrouded in a thick financial fog, sprang from artificially invented complex investment instruments so far beyond industry norms that not even the most astute bankers and economists fully understood them. Only full transparency can disperse such a fog.

Transparency matters because in the real world of accelerated change *nothing* ever goes as planned. Count on it. Surviving during a time of dramatic change demands visibility; thriving on it demands perfect visibility. The Great Recession blindsided us because only a few unheeded voices warned about the iceberg looming over the bow of our titanic economy.

A business that cannot see its problems will sink. In the NOW organization, the Quarterly Target Review (QTR) makes problems clearly visible to everyone, and thus provides a pivotal tool for maintaining transparency. A formal review of work *in* and *on* the business, the QTR trains a microscope on the business, revealing any gaps between targets and actual performance. It clears and focuses the lens. It reinforces accountability in a way that makes people feel safe when they voice their concerns. Ideally, the reviews occur at every level of the organization, as process and initiative owners and those accountable for overseeing and measuring progress share their results and seek help solving problems.

The QTR not only enables you to make planned, periodic adjustments to work *on* and *in* the business, it also paves the way for the total transparency that keeps a business humming in the now. By removing fear from the equation, it solves all of the major problems that can hold a company back from hitting its targets. Fear of criticism, fear of failure, fear of embarrassment, and fear of *not* doing your part can prevent the openness and honesty it takes to solve problems at the speed of now. True, fear is a natural part of life, but organizations that play on fear and shame cause their employees to bury problems underground. Managers who engender fear will stunt the energy and creativity of the vast majority of people who work for them. Fear slams on the brake, slowing everything down to a crawl as everyone keeps a wary eye on their backside, instead of putting their energy and time into solving problems.

It would take an entire book to examine all the ways by which leaders can install a culture of transparency in their organization. Indeed, many of the tools presented in this book relate to transparency; but in this chapter we focus on one of the most important: the review process.

Waiting for the end of the year to review outcome and process measures, as well as the status of breakthrough initiatives, can thwart efforts to run your business effectively. Therefore, you need to do them more often. Some processes and some initiatives may require hourly, weekly, and monthly monitoring, but you should formally review major ones every three months.

The Quarterly Target Review creates a forum in which transparency rules. Its structure and the behaviors it promotes will, over time, permeate the daily operating life in the NOW organization. It also will set in motion the dynamics that will lead the organization from the traditional dreaded "annual employee performance review" to real-time, action-oriented feedback for every NOW worker. In the final section of this chapter you will see an example of real-time organizational transparency, where everyone sees obstacles and solves problems at the speed of now.

Getting the Transparency Train on Track

"Well, thank you very much, we appreciate that . . . asshole," blurted Enron Chief Operating Officer Jeffrey Skilling, reacting to assertions by analyst Richard Gruman, of Highfield Capital, that Enron had falsified its financial statements. Gruman had discovered that Enron's Chief Financial Officer Andrew Fastow and his team had been using offshore entities to move currency and hide losses at an organization that *Fortune* magazine had, for six consecutive years, dubbed "America's Most Innovative Company." Innovative, indeed!

The rest is history. Plunging from the pinnacle of greed and opulence to the black pit of bankruptcy, Enron became the poster child for total lack of corporate transparency because of its "innovative accounting practices."

In behind-the-scenes board meetings and management sessions, Skilling and Fastow had created an aura of creativity and managerial brilliance, masked as complex business acumen. One board member, an engineer by training, resigned when Enron's accounting and finance methods grew so baffling he could not comprehend them.

Transparency makes such deception impossible. QTRs promote transparency by providing public forums for thorough peer review and discussion of what's actually going on in the business. If people don't understand something, they probe until they "get it." If something doesn't make sense, they can safely question the situation until the pieces come together.

To be effective, the QTR must take place in an environment of complete safety. That safety sets the right tone and sends a clear message for how this company does business, inside and out. People must feel comfortable expressing their honest opinions—especially about problems, obstacles, and setbacks—even if doing so reveals that they

RULES FOR TOTAL TRANSPARENCY

1. Seek facts not blame.

2. Ask for and offer help.

3. Speak the truth, respectfully.

4. Think organizationally act departmentally.

5. Engage fully.

6. Laugh and play.

7. Share leadership.

FIGURE 7.1   Seven Rules for Total Transparency

themselves made an error in judgment or failed to get something done. NOW organizations incorporate Seven Rules for Total Transparency (Figure 7.1) into *everything* they do, especially their review meetings.

RULE 1: SEEK FACTS NOT BLAME

A well-run QTR takes the guesswork out of problem solving by focusing on facts rather than opinions and unsubstantiated theories. Of course, the same applies to all work in a NOW organization. Solutions depend on cold, hard facts. Concentrating on the facts helps remove emotion and resist the tendency to lay blame when discussing a business problem. If a sales manager points out problems with the accounts receivable system, everyone can examine the facts without laying blame on the accounting department. If a team lacks sufficient facts to explore solutions to the problem, then they will conduct more research before moving forward. (Chapter 8 provides a step-by-step problem-solving methodology based on the facts of a situation.)

RULE 2: ASK FOR AND OFFER HELP

The QTR gives everyone a chance to offer one another support, the hallmark of a healthy business. Asking for and offering help builds an atmosphere of solidarity. Sometimes people feel reluctant to ask for help, falsely thinking that doing so will make them look weak or ill informed. In fact, it signifies wisdom. Wise people know they don't know everything, and can't do it all by themselves. By the same token, most people feel flattered when someone asks for their help.

For example, Bonnie, highly skilled in the use of social media, can help accountant Robert develop a speedier way to follow up on delinquent accounts. Robert can help Bonnie understand cash flow, and thus solve a problem with a delinquent customer account. Instead of two wary people thrown together on a project, they become two colleagues who like and trust each other.

RULE 3: SPEAK THE TRUTH, RESPECTFULLY

Sometimes the truth hurts, but falsehoods and cover-ups do even greater harm. Never bury the truth, no matter how painful. That said, when you speak the truth, do so with the utmost respect. Everyone then learns and grows. Remember, as well, to share good news and praise good work.

Choose your words carefully. If Robert admits discomfort using social media to stay in touch with accounts, Bonnie should resist the urge to say, "Oh, it's so easy, my kid can do it." Instead, she might admit to Robert, "Look, it took me forever to get comfortable with it, but now I really love it."

And when someone's disrespectful behavior in a QTR threatens another's sense of safety, others should feel free to point that out. Persistent threatening behavior requires intervention outside the meeting, where it will not distract from the business at hand and where the offender will not be embarrassed in front of colleagues. If, for example, Bonnie tends to offend people with her unintentionally dismissive remarks, Robert might bring that to her attention in a one-on-one chat at lunch. Or if Robert openly accuses Bonnie of incompetence in the meeting, a colleague should object immediately. Both situations require tact, as well as respect. Truth-telling and respect go a long way toward canceling fear and building trust.

RULE 4: THINK ORGANIZATIONALLY, ACT DEPARTMENTALLY

People quite naturally tend to think in terms of what's best for their own departments, but in a NOW organization they always balance their departmental concerns with what best serves the organization. That holds true especially when people see their work within the context of boundary-crossing processes rather than departmental silos. This view ensures that departments support the success of the organization. A strong silo in a weak organization will eventually fail. Likewise, a strong organization with a weak department will eventually pay a price for that shortcoming.

Bonnie's social media expertise will accomplish nothing if a serious problem in accounting puts the company in financial jeopardy. Not even the most effective accounting system can save a company that does not learn to do *business at the speed of now.*

RULE 5: ENGAGE FULLY

Just as everyone should think both departmentally and organizationally, they also should view everything not only from their individual perspective but from the perspective of the CEO or team leader. Full engagement requires empathy with those above, below, and around you. When you are fully engaged, you freely display interest, express concern, seek and offer help, make suggestions, ask questions, probe for details, and congratulate accomplishment. Fully engaged individuals do not wait for a problem to worsen before they offer help; they volunteer the instant they see the problem.

When Bonnie sees Robert fully engaged in the work and the enterprise, she feels motivated to do likewise. In this way, full engagement unites the team and motivates everyone to do their best to solve problems and hit their targets. Everyone wants to be part of a great team, and a single fully engaged teammate improves everyone's game.

RULE 6: LAUGH AND PLAY

People often approach the review process with a certain amount of tension, and even apprehension. Regardless of the seriousness of a problem, however, you tend to solve it more quickly and creatively if you lighten up and find some humor in the situation. Certainly, work may offer daunting challenges, but they are seldom matters of life and death. Solutions tend to retreat when you attack them with deadly seriousness, but surrender naturally and spontaneously when approached with lighthearted playfulness.

People also feel safer in a more lighthearted environment. True to the old stereotype, accountant Robert tends to frown a lot when he sees disappointing numbers, whereas Bonnie's infectious laughter always brings a smile to his face. The humor they increasingly share has led to more than a few "Eureka" moments that might never had occurred if they approached every problem as if someone would suffer a loss.

RULE 7: SHARE LEADERSHIP

As Emmett Murphy stressed in his groundbreaking book, *Leadership IQ*, "Every leader works, and every worker leads." Everyone in the organization should take accountability for modeling the ground rules, regardless of who actually chairs a meeting or runs a department or owns a process. While it may take more time for shy Robert to speak up and share his honest opinions, it comes quite easily to gregarious Bonnie.

Certain situations can cause people to ignore or even act contrary to the rules that govern behavior in a transparent organization. Major surprises in the business environment or the competitive arena, unexpected internal crises, or the loss of a key colleague in the midst of a major initiative can instill fear. Nothing threatens transparency more than fear, which prompts one of three classic responses: freeze, flee, or fight, illustrated in Figure 7.2. When the tiger pops out of the jungle, inaction will almost always turn you into tiger food, and running away will only delay the inevitable, so you might as well

FIGURE 7.2 Reactions to Fear

fight to solve the problem. Fully engaged teammates greatly increase the odds in your favor.

In a 1965 paper titled "Developmental Sequence in Small Groups" by Bruce Tuckman, published in *Psychological Bulletin*, Tuckman introduced an excellent model of group performance that describes the predictable stages through which a group progresses as it forms or reforms. It applies particularly well to organizational transparency:

Forming: Team members begin, however cautiously or reluctantly, to get along with each other. When Robert first joins the team, he worries about how people will treat him; in contrast, Bonnie clearly enjoys getting to know new people. It takes time for the two of them to feel comfortable with each other.

Storming: Teammates let down the politeness barrier and try to get down to the issues, even if a situation causes emotions to spike. Robert initially misinterprets Bonnie's frequent laughter as her way of poking fun at his seriousness. When he angrily confronts her, she initially responds in kind, but soon apologizes and explains her natural tendency to see the funny side of an issue.

Norming: People grow more familiar with each other, develop trust, and begin to establish productive work patterns. Bonnie and Robert gradually become friends, sharing details of their personal lives (Robert offers anecdotes about his three kids; Bonnie admits that she feels a little nervous about her second marriage). Over time, they develop a relationship that goes beyond the necessities of work. They accomplish more and more as they begin to know what to expect from each other and join forces to solve problems.

Performing: The team efficiently and cooperatively works as a group toward a common goal. Now Robert and Bonnie really get humming as teammates. They enjoy each other's company and welcome each and every opportunity to hit their targets. Not surprisingly, they turn in target-beating results.

Awareness of these evolving stages will help you understand what to expect in the organization as a whole, as well as in the business reviews. The QTRs set the tone for overall transparency because they provide the forum where people examine and discuss everything that's going on in the organization. A healthy NOW business performs far better than its competitors because it lives and thrives on transparency, a transparency that encourages people to face the challenges of running the business so they can quickly and effectively address them.

Initiating Transparency with Business Reviews

Why does transparency matter? Because lies generate fear, and nothing paralyzes people in an organization more than fear. When the boss makes it clear that she will not tolerate mistakes, punishing anyone who does not live up to her expectations, people avoid telling her the truth or openly admitting their mistakes. Such an environment inevitably leads to secrecy, finger-pointing, cover-ups, and, in the extreme, outright lying. In a culture built on transparency, leaders do not use accountability as a hammer. When motivational leaders in transparent organizations say, "We will hold ourselves accountable for results," people know they mean, "We will work together to figure out this problem, own responsibility for solving it, develop good solutions, and get the job done." Those words do not punish, they motivate.

Lack of transparency and the misuse of accountability paralyze people; and paralyzed people cannot do their best work, much less function at the speed of now. Transparency and accountability go hand in hand. Their opposites, secrecy and blame, devastate performance. In Chapter 9, we'll look more closely at the harmful consequences of fear in an organization. Here we will examine how eliminating it begins with the way you analyze progress toward targeted results.

During an organization's transition from *then* to *now*, its leaders must install a system for analyzing progress that tells the unvarnished truth about what's really happening in the organization. That truth creates transparency. The Quarterly Target Review gets the ball rolling in the right direction. This public forum highlights and reinforces new behaviors, new thinking, and new levels of maturity. It not only sets a tone, it establishes a necessary set of business disciplines that prepare and enable people to function comfortably and confidently at the speed of now.

The QTR probes business performance in great detail. It takes place in a completely safe environment, where people take

QUARTERLY TARGET REVIEWS

FIGURE **7.3**   Target Reviews

accountability, talk openly about the obstacles that are getting in the way of planned performance, and determine corrective actions that will ensure the best possible outcomes.

Disciplined, well-crafted QTRs set the stage for addressing all of the problems in the business as it moves toward its objectives. The best QTRs:

- ◆ Assess the status of overall performance-to-targets for:
  - Outcome measures
  - Process measures
  - Performance breakthroughs
  - Capability breakthroughs
- ◆ Report the facts surrounding the root causes of performance shortfalls.
- ◆ Specify the implications of deviations from plans.
- ◆ Propose plans to address the root causes of the shortfalls.
- ◆ Emphasize leadership's commitment to achieve their goals.

In addition, well-executed QTRs greatly affect the behavior of those accountable for results, because they:

- ◆ Reinforce discipline, accountability, and the importance of taking effective action.
- ◆ Enable all involved to share the joy of accomplishment.
- ◆ Keep everyone focused on results.
- ◆ Motivate people to take effective action before and after the review.
- ◆ Instill confidence and hope.

The following discussion of QTRs assumes an organization has been using them for 9 to 18 months, depending upon organization size and leadership discipline. It takes that long for the review process to cascade from the top to the bottom of an organization.

Immediately after the quarter has ended, teams at various levels in the organization gather all relevant data about the performance of their fundamentals and breakthroughs, updating their scorecards, generating any Fundamental Improvement Plans (we'll describe how to create these in Chapter 8), and completing Breakthrough Status Reviews (Chapter 6). As they conduct their business reviews, teams decide which perform-ance issues, if any, should escalate to the next level of the organization. In some cases, an issue may remain with the team; in others, it may progress no further than the departmental or process level; in still others, it may work its way all the way up to senior leadership. It all depends on how confidently the team itself can tackle the issue.

At every level, participants talk openly and honestly about all obstacles and opportunities, following the Seven Rules for Total Trans-parency. Note that the chart in Figure 7.4 is illustrative. An organization might label the second level up from the front-line teams as "processes" or "departments," using whatever terminology is appropriate.

Because QTRs embody the principle of truth telling, they reinforce the organization's values, stimulate new, more productive behaviors, and supply leaders with a powerful culture-building tool. This tool helps them create an environment in which people feel fired up to do what it takes to get results with focus, discipline, and determination. No

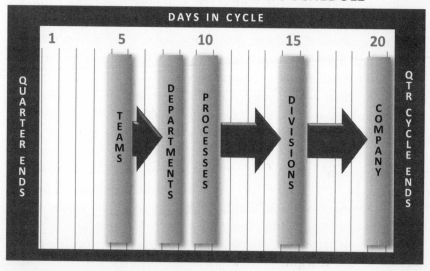

FIGURE **7.4** Target Review Schedule

other leadership action in the early stages of the transformation to *now* will do more to ensure the proper allocation of precious resources. With that in mind, let's walk through the QTR process one step at a time.

Preparing for Target Reviews

Larry Bossidy, former chairman and CEO of Honeywell International, wrote in the introduction to his book *Execution: The Discipline of Getting Things Done*, "By the time I retired—after the merger with Honeywell in 1999—we had tripled our operating margins to almost 15 percent, raised our return on equity from just over 10 percent to 28 percent, and delivered an almost ninefold return to shareholders. How did we do it? We created a discipline of execution."

His coauthor, business advisor Ram Charan, added, "Execution is *the* great unaddressed issue in the business world today." What does he mean by "execution?" "Execution is not just tactics—it's a discipline and a system. It has to be built into a company's strategy, its goals, and its culture."

QTRs add the discipline Bossidy and Charan recommend because QTRs analyze progress and help leaders make important decisions about adjusting actions and reallocating resources in order to stay on plan.

Before you tackle your initial QTR, you need to establish a policy that governs taking corrective action driven by shortfalls in performance measures and initiatives. You also must carefully prepare the content and agenda for the meeting and make sure all participants grasp the importance of a rigorous review.

A corrective action policy defines when and how owners will make necessary midcourse adjustments in order to execute the plan effectively. The policy defines the conditions that should prompt the organization to take corrective action. By specifying *who, when,* and *what,* it reinforces the accountability of every individual, team, department, and division of the business to make adjustments that will get the plan back on track. Emphasizing a practical process for taking corrective action, the policy assigns *authority* to take action based on facts and hard data, and it clarifies *how* to take action using Seven-Step Problem Solving and Breakthrough Status Reviews.

Take a look in Figure 7.5 at what our illustrative firm, BearPaw, developed as its Improvement Policy.

BearPawsoft.com

Improvement Guidelines

GUIDELINE

An Outcome Measure or a Process Measure (a.k.a. a Fundamental) or a Breakthrough Plan will move into corrective action when the owner of that measure or plan determines a need for intervention to support the achievement of the current Operating Plan. A Fundamental or a Breakthrough in either a "red" or "yellow" status with "declining" or "stable" trend requires formal action to improve its performance.

The improvement process requires removing the Fundamental or Breakthrough from normal day-to-day management, and allocating the additional resources needed to get it back on track.

PROCESS

1. The owner of an Outcome Measure, Process Measure, or Breakthrough Plan notifies management that there is a performance issue, and that the Fundamental or the Breakthrough is moving into corrective action for improvement.

2. Within 10 working days, the owner initiates a Fundamental Improvement Plan or a Breakthrough Status Review to identify appropriate action steps to improve performance.

3. Within 20 days, the improvement planning work is complete and the implementation of corrective action is underway.

4. The owner and his or her manager agree upon the frequency of updates, ranging from daily to monthly depending on the criticality and urgency of the improvement needed.

5. Once the owner has achieved improvements that demonstrate measurable gains and "green" status, the Fundamental or Breakthrough returns to normal management processes.

SUPPORTING DOCUMENTS

1. Fundamental Improvement Plan
2. Breakthrough Status Review

FIGURE **7.5** BearPaw's Improvement Policy

BearPaw's leaders communicate that they want people to take corrective action whenever performance measures fall below expectations, or initiatives are struggling to meet plan. Action depends on hard facts and numbers, not feelings and suspicions. People associated with the measure or the initiative should figure out exactly what's causing the shortfall and then devise a plan to get back on track.

To ensure a well-organized meeting, create a QTR Preparation Checklist, such as this one, that covers all the important bases:

1. Have we gathered all relevant data for all outcome and process scorecards?
2. Have we collected Fundamental Improvement Plans for underperforming outcomes and processes? (See Chapter 8.)
3. Have we collected Breakthrough Status Reviews for all initiatives?
4. Have we published a well-organized and complete agenda for the meeting?

You want to do everything you can to prevent surprises during the QTR, especially someone presenting unsettling facts no one has yet seen. Unexpected bad news can shock or embarrass people and ignite the fear that can compromise transparency.

Real-Time Transparency and Corrective Action

"Brace for impact!"

On the morning of January 15, 2009, Chesley "Sully" Sullenberger, the captain of US Airways Flight 1549, uttered the words no pilot wants to say and no passenger wants to hear. Moments earlier, his Airbus A320 had collided with a large flock of birds, forcing the aircraft's engines to shut down. Sullenberger made the split-second decision to ditch the aircraft and its 155 passengers in the Hudson River.

Sullenberger himself credited his training and his expert knowledge of flight safety and the causes of plane crashes, not his nerves, for saving the day. Training, knowledge, and practice save the day in a NOW organization.

While investigating the causes of plane crashes may seem a far cry from Quarterly Target Reviews, the two activities share similarities. Both rely on facts, both look for root causes, and both dictate corrective actions to prevent unwanted results. More importantly, both enable the quick and effective decision making needed to operate at the speed of now.

QTRs give teams a disciplined way to stop, look, listen, and decide. As people grow accustomed to using them to review progress and take corrective action, they integrate that thinking into their daily decision-making process. They quickly react in a disciplined way to any opportunity or problem that presents itself. That's what Captain Sullenberger did. While he spent untold hours acquiring the skills and knowledge a pilot needs to do his job, when a problem presented itself, he reacted swiftly and effectively.

Business at the speed of now becomes a reality when everyone in the organization responds swiftly and effectively every minute of every workday. A customer presents an unusual problem? A new product contains a minor, but fatal, flaw? A competitor introduces a game-changing feature that renders your offering obsolete? Get the facts, take ownership and accountability, and solve it *now*.

Just as airline pilots need a complete and fully functioning cockpit instrument panel (dashboard) in order to make all the snap decisions that will enable them to move their cargo and passengers safely to their final destination, NOW workers need a complete and fully functioning system that gives them real-time data on the performance of both their routine work and their contributions to breakthrough initiatives.

Imagine: When "Brandy Cochran" comes to work each day at BearPaw, she immediately logs into her personal NOW Inside (see Figure 7.6). This dashboard gives her an at-a-glance update on everything she needs to know in order to do her work at the speed of now. She can click on any of her measures and see her performance history, the red/yellow/green ranges, and her target. She quickly determines the challenges that demand her attention.

On NOW Inside, Brandy looks at her FUNDAMENTALS, her basic accountabilities, and the color coding to determine how well the things she is accountable for are going. If an area requires corrective action, this is indicated by the box next to the measure being in red or yellow. If it does need action, she clicks on the "Create a 7-Step Plan" link to create a Fundamental Improvement Plan, connects it to the measure, and goes to work on her plan. Clicking to MY TEAM, Brandy checks in to see how the rest of her team is doing on the same measure—or any other measure, for that matter. With each click she can easily follow her measure up through her team, her process, her

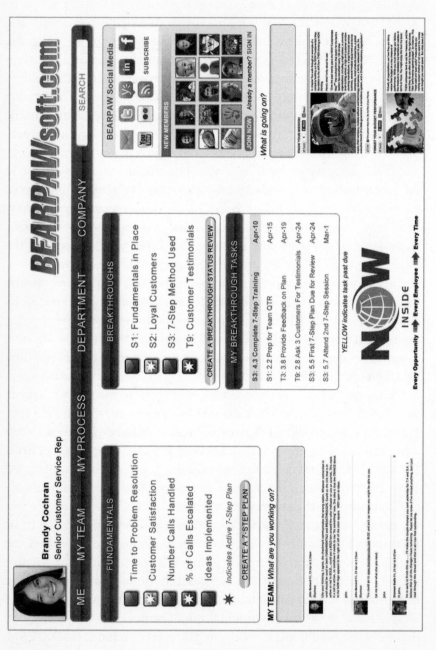

FIGURE 7.6 NOW Inside Example for BearPaw

department, and, ultimately, to the top level of the business. Connecting the impact her work has on the company delights Brandy, because it shows that her work really does make a difference.

Still on NOW Inside, Katy performs the same status-at-a-glance for her BREAKTHROUGHS, viewing all her assigned tasks in due-date order so she always knows exactly when she needs to accomplish a given deliverable. Whenever she clicks on a breakthrough, she can read the complete Breakthrough Plan, scour the details in the Breakthrough Workplan, or examine any archived existing Breakthrough Status Review. If she needs to create a new Breakthrough Status Review, Katy can start it with one click.

Because Katy Cochran can always see what her company needs from her, and continuously assess how she's doing and where she needs to concentrate her attention, she can confidently seize opportunities and solve problems. Throughout the day she relies on social media and cloud computing to get the facts, make vital connections, and communicate with colleagues, customers, and, when necessary, company managers and leaders. She researches the competition by accessing relevant industry blogs. She lends a hand whenever a teammate or someone from a different department sends her an instant message requesting information or an answer to a nettlesome question. She scans coworkers' internal "Facebook" pages to identify an individual whose expertise and experience might help *her* solve a problem. In this mature state of real-time visibility Brandy will find it quite easy to prepare for the QTR because she has been dealing with QTR issues every day. And since her dashboard lets her continually monitor her performance and initiatives, she can enter the QTR with full confidence that she is on top of the important issues.

Managers and leaders may recognize accountability and transparency when they see it, but they must bring those concepts to life by demonstrating them with their own behavior. They can conduct business reviews following the Seven Rules of Total Transparency. They can show their people how they themselves recognize a problem, take ownership and accountability for it, design an effective solution, and put that solution to work. The same applies to honesty and trust. You can't achieve it overnight. It takes time. But all that time and effort will pay off big-time when everyone in your organization finally operates at the speed of now.

Transparency might have prevented the shocking fall of Lehman Brothers. Its leaders would have seen the early-warning signs that they were heading into an iceberg. More importantly, they would have steered their company away from those bad decisions in the first place.

■ ■ ■

Complete the Speedometer for Creating NOW Transparency (Table 7.1) and add your net score to the summary sheet in the Appendix.

TABLE 7.1   NOW Speedometer 7: Creating NOW Transparency

Then	−1	0	+1	Now
We don't conduct formal business reviews				We use business reviews to drive action and improve organizational performance
We don't safely or effectively review business performance				We make our business reviews safe and effective
We do not involve every employee in some form of business review				We involve every employee in our business reviews
We don't carefully prepare for formal business reviews				We thoroughly prepare for business reviews
We expect management to guide corrective action when plans go off track				We make sure every employee can take corrective action to keep plans on track
We don't use technology to ensure transparency and drive corrective action				We use technology to maintain transparency and drive corrective action
We review performance annually				We review performance continually
Subtotals				
NOW Transparency **NET SCORE**				

Add this score to the consolidated score in the Appendix.

SPEEDOMETER

THEN		NOW

−7 −6 −5 −4 −3 −2 −1 |0| +1 +2 +3 +4 +5 +6 +7

Solving Problems Now

Equip Everyone with the Core Skill

At 11:38 AM on an unusually cold January morning in 1986, a worldwide television audience thrilled at the sight of the space shuttle *Challenger* soaring into the bright blue Florida sky. Seconds later, millions watched in horror as the spacecraft, carrying civilian passenger, New Hampshire schoolteacher Christa McAuliffe, exploded and disintegrated before their eyes. The catastrophe not only shocked the world, it brought NASA's shuttle program to a standstill for more than 32 months.

What caused the catastrophe? The failure of an inexpensive, dime-sized rubber O-ring manufactured by Morton-Thiokol. At a televised hearing, theoretical physicist Richard Feynman, a member of the Rogers Commission charged with determining the root cause of the disaster, famously demonstrated how the O-rings became less resilient and subject to seal failures at ice-cold temperatures by immersing a sample of the material in a glass of ice water.

The commission's report also criticized the failure of both NASA and Morton-Thiokol management to respond adequately to the danger posed by the flawed O-ring. Rather than redesigning the joint that the O-ring should have sealed properly, they deemed the problem an acceptable flight risk. The report found that NASA managers had known about the flawed design as early as 1977 but never discussed the problem outside their reporting channels with Morton-Thiokol, a flagrant violation of NASA regulations and processes. Even when the seriousness of the flaw became apparent, no one at NASA considered grounding the shuttles until a fix could be implemented. On the contrary, managers waived six launch constraints related to the O-rings, and that decision led to a disaster that left a permanent and horrific image of *Challenger's* explosion in the minds of all who watched that day.

The incident illustrates the potential hazard when well-meaning people fail to step in and solve a seemingly little problem. Problems, both big and small, abound in all organizations, and even the little ones, in the blink of an eye, can become big. That's why NOW organizations emphasize speedy and sure problem solving at every level, giving every employee the freedom and tools to make decisions now.

As with all aspects of doing *business at the speed of now*, an organization must develop a common language and shared toolset. That way, anyone who becomes involved in solving a problem can immediately get up to speed and work effectively and efficiently with teammates, no matter which department or process they represent, and no matter their position in the organization. The CEO can walk into a meeting of maintenance personnel and immediately see the status of a problem-solving effort; likewise, someone from accounting can observe colleagues in marketing as they work on a problem with brand development and know just how far they need to go before they can implement a solution.

In the case of the *Challenger* disaster, the O-ring failure was not the root cause of the problem. No; the root cause was the lack of a well-defined and widely understood problem-solving methodology that would have assured that even the failure of a tiny O-ring would receive swift and sure attention. Nowadays you can select from an array of proven problem-solving tools, such as process maps, cause-and-effect diagrams, check sheets, histograms, and Pareto analyses. In this chapter, however, we focus on Mass Ingenuity's Seven-Step Problem-Solving methodology and demonstrate how a team at a computer chip manufacturer might use it to solve a serious business problem. Our methodology gives individuals and teams a simple, versatile tool they can apply to both simple and complicated problems.

We developed this methodology to solve problems with an organization's routine processes, such as excessive overtime, declining productivity of a particular process, slow product development, or sagging customer satisfaction scores. We do not recommend it for overarching strategic problems such as reacting to a major threat from a competitor or acquiring and nurturing the talent you need to make a major breakthrough (achieving breakthroughs was covered in Chapter 6).

Creating the Charter

"Anita Houser," the frustrated CEO of "Matrix Semiconductor" called us because she needed help with a problem in the company's manufacturing process. "We produce a chipset for smartphones," she explained. "Suddenly almost 10 percent of our chipsets are failing final test. That's causing us to miss delivery dates to customers who cannot afford the delays."

Matrix began the year with an optimistic projection of 25 to 30 percent growth in a fast-growing industry, where sales of smartphones were predicted to reach 1.2 billion units globally. Suppliers were rushing to fill that demand. Matrix itself was running full tilt, three shifts a day, seven days a week to supply phone manufacturers with crucial chipsets, but somehow its complex highly automated production line was not smoothly churning out the 700,000 units per week the company needed to produce to hit its growth targets.

When we asked for more specifics about the problem, Anita told us that with the failure rate hovering near 10 percent, the company was losing valuable time making replacements. The strain on the Matrix production process had led to an almost two-day delay in shipping orders to customers. Once happy customers were growing impatient and threatening to take their business elsewhere. Since Anita's team had not been able to get things back on track quickly enough, she felt an outside consultant might help.

We suggested that she consider using our Seven-Step Problem-Solving method in this situation as shown in Figure 8.1, confident it would not only help her people get to the bottom of this particular issue quickly, but would also give them a permanent new tool they could use every day in their routine work.

Seven-Step Problem Solving

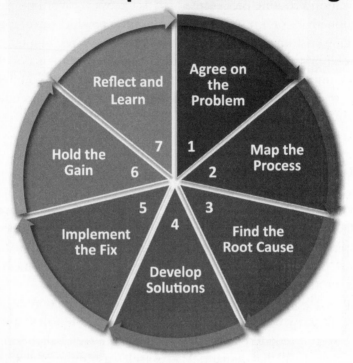

FIGURE 8.1   Seven Steps to Solve Problems

First we worked with Anita to create a charter for the team, an essential element in any effort to solve a cross-functional problem like the one plaguing Matrix. A good charter includes:

Team Charter
a. A preliminary problem statement.
b. The current level of performance.
c. The desired level of performance.
d. The consequences of not solving the problem.
e. The sponsor(s) of the project.
f. A project leader and team members (from each of the relevant functions).
g. A project completion date.

Anita drafted a concise problem statement: "The unusually high failure rate of our chipsets is causing us to miss our delivery date commitments to customers." She added the current level of performance (9.6 percent failures; deliveries shipped an average 36 hours late) and the desired level (.5 percent failures; deliveries on time). What consequences could befall Matrix if the company fails to solve the problem? If only six customers switch to a more reliable supplier, the company will go out of business.

Anita herself will sponsor the project. She assigns Brad Ritter, the manager in charge of chipset packaging, to lead the team. He is skilled at solving problems, a talent he developed when he worked for a former client five years ago, at which time he received training in Seven-Step Problem Solving from Mass Ingenuity. Anita adds five more people to the team, each with a different and important perspective on the problem, and each well respected by his or her peers:

Aditya Patnaik, a manufacturing engineer from chip fabrication

Maria Sanchez, a test engineer from chip testing

David Rauch, an assembler from chip packaging

Billie Jo Jenkins, a materials expediter

Xui Li, a quality engineer

Anita sets the target for project completion as "within 48 hours."

With the charter in hand, Anita gathers the team for its first session. She projects the Seven-Step Problem-Solving chart on a 50-inch flat-screen monitor at the front of the meeting room.

Step 1: Agree on the Problem

Achieve team consensus on the definition of the problem, including the reasons for solving it as quickly as possible, how to measure success, and a tentative deadline. Aim for a concise, clear, blame-free statement that does not suggest solutions.

RULES FOR TOTAL TRANSPARENCY

1. Seek facts not blame.

2. Ask for and offer help.

3. Speak the truth respectfully.

4. Think organizationally act departmentally.

5. Engage fully.

6. Laugh and play.

7. Share leadership.

FIGURE 8.2   Transparency Rules

Most, if not all, of the team already know about the problem, and many bring a certain amount of "baggage" to the initial meeting. Anita reviews the Seven Rules for Total Transparency (introduced in Chapter 7 and shown again in Figure 8.2), stressing the need for everyone to leave their prejudices, preconceptions, and pet theories at the door.

Anita then turns the meeting over to Brad, who emphasizes the reasons for assembling this team. "As Anita pointed out, we must fix this problem, or Matrix will start losing customers. There are a lot of aggressive competitors out there just waiting for us to stumble."

After Brad guides the group through a review of Anita's preliminary problem statement, everyone agrees that they should rewrite it using more precise language. They revise it to read: "9.6 percent of chipsets are failing final test, causing us to miss delivery commitments by 36 hours on average, thus jeopardizing our customers' financial results."

They debate the target that Anita set when she drafted the original problem statement: 48 hours to set in motion a solution that will lead back to a .5 percent failure rate and on-time deliveries. While most like the goals, the engineers, Aditya Patnaik and Maria Sanchez, point out that it might take more time to implement a solution. Brad concurs: "No point in setting an unrealistic deadline that will drive us crazy." Eventually, the team agrees to add 24 hours, for a total of 72.

Brad claps his hands. "Okay folks, let's get to work and map out the process."

Step 2: Map the Process

Understand how the work currently gets done and where it breaks down. Create a process map, or maps, of the related processes, including all decision points.

No single person on the team fully understands the complete end-to-end process for building a chipset. Maria knows how testing fits into the picture, but she has not spent much time on the assembly line watching David do his job. The company has grown rapidly in the past three years and now employs 1,500 people, with dozens more coming on board each month. It takes time to learn the whole process, and without that luxury in this case, Anita has chosen this particular group because each person can add a crucial piece to the puzzle. Once everyone can see the whole picture, they will know what data they need to collect about the current problem.

The team starts with a high-level, or "bird's-eye view," process map, because that will give everyone the simplest and most understandable overview of the process. They title the process "Fab-to-Final Test," which includes everything that occurs from the moment an order arrives from a customer to shipment to that customer. When Brad asks the team to list the functions involved between the beginning and end points, they agree on these five:

- Fabrication (which assembles the chips)
- Chip Testing (which initially tests for quality)
- Materials (which pulls parts required for packaging the tested chip)

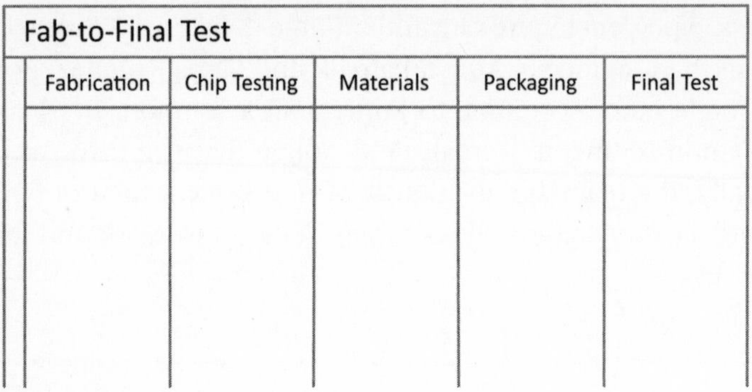

Fab-to-Final Test				
Fabrication	Chip Testing	Materials	Packaging	Final Test

FIGURE **8.3**　Matrix's Starting Process Map

- ◆ Packaging (which assembles the chip and other components and then seals the assembly in a plastic package)
- ◆ Final Test (which determines whether Matrix can ship the packages).

The Fabrication, Chip Testing, Materials, Packaging, and Final Test columns on the process map look like the swim lanes in an Olympic pool, as shown in Figure 8.3.

In this case, the team draws the map on a large sheet of paper tacked to the wall, and uses sticky notes to add ideas and suggestions of how the process currently works to each "swim lane." Engineer Aditya scribbles a note and sticks it under Fabrication; Maria adds a couple under Chip Testing; David sticks one below Aditya's; Billie Jo puts several on the board under Materials, and Li sticks one under Chip Testing and two under Final Test. Within an hour the board bristles with a few dozen multicolored sticky notes. The elaborate chip fabrication process involves more than 150 steps, but at this point the team maintains their high-level view; they do not attempt to add every single detail. Later, after they have collected data related key decision points, they can include more details if necessary. Wisely, they avoid jumping to any conclusions at this stage, even though everyone suspects that the problem does not start with the unassembled chipset. Brad now guides the team to consolidate all those sticky notes into a simple high-level process map (see Figure 8.4).

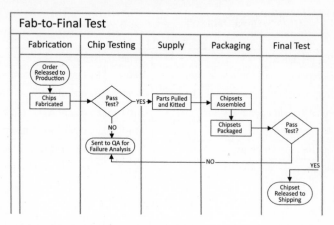

Fab-to-Final Test

| Fabrication | Chip Testing | Supply | Packaging | Final Test |

FIGURE **8.4** Matrix's High-Level Process Map

With this map in hand, the team can now move to step 3. Brad reminds the team that once they have collected sufficient data about these swim lanes they will almost surely come back to this stage and create a more detailed map of one of this map's subprocesses. "But we have enough of a feel for the big picture, and we can start looking for possible root causes."

Step 3: Find the Root Cause

Gather the data needed to understand how and why the process breaks down. Complete a root cause analysis and list all likely suspects.

A lot of informal theories had occurred to people well before the team took this next step. David from assembly thinks one of the chips coming out of fabrication may contain a flaw because a similar problem occurred six months earlier. Xui from quality wonders if the chip might suffer damage between the point at which they are put into kits and the point at which they travel from fabrication to packaging. Aditya, the manufacturing engineer, chalks it up to a bug in the final test software. Theories abound, but then theories are just guesses based on opinions rather than facts. To find the real root cause, the team needs to get all the facts.

TABLE **8.1** Matrix's Suspect Data Log

Suspect Data Log			
Item	Data Needed	Owner	Details
1	Number of chips fabricated (step 2)	Aditya	By day of week and by shift
2	Number of chipsets packaged (step 7)	David	By day of week and by shift
3	Percent yield at chip test	Maria	By day of week and by shift
4	Percent yield at final test	David	By day of week and by shift
5	Failure type for chips	Xui	Cause of failure after analysis
6	Failure type for chipsets	Xui	Cause of failure after analysis

The team uses the process map they built to brainstorm the data they need to collect. In particular, they look at the decision points in each process (the diamond-shaped boxes in the map), because they mark additional points at which the process can break down. Like good detectives, the team wants to create a list of likely suspects, in descending order of probability. They can then collect and analyze evidence about those potential culprits.

Together, they come up with a strong list of suspects, itemized in Table 8.1. Focusing on the most likely ones, they identify six initial pieces of data they think will give them the best overview of what has been going on in the factory over the past several weeks. Naturally, each team member knows a lot about his or her area of responsibility, so individuals take ownership for certain data.

Finishing up the session, the team breaks so that everyone can collect the required data before reconvening the next morning at 8:00 AM. That allows plenty of time to do a thorough job.

The next morning, each person responsible for gathering an important piece of the puzzle presents his or her findings to the team, in the form of charts displaying facts and figures for the past few weeks. The team turns its attention to the third item, percent yield at chip test, and notes that the numbers do not support any theories about a possible glitch in the fabrication process.

Then, when David presents the figures for percent yield at final test, an interesting fact emerges. Something clearly went wrong during the Saturday evening shift a little over a week ago, when percent yield tumbled to 92.88 and stayed low from that point onward (see Table 8.2).

TABLE 8.2   Percent Yield at Final Test

	Day	Swing	Graveyard
Monday	99.12	99.22	99.33
Tuesday	98.88	98.83	99.22
Wednesday	99.22	98.97	99.12
Thursday	98.98	99.12	98.88
Friday	99.01	98.88	99.01
Saturday	99.03	98.35	92.88
Sunday	90.13	91.40	90.88
Monday	89.89	90.97	91.30
Tuesday	90.56	89.03	92.10
Wednesday	91.20	90.77	91.11
Thursday	92.90	93.20	92.90
Friday	91.40	93.50	91.40
Saturday	90.97	92.90	90.97

This may break the case wide open. David quickly draws a chart (Figure 8.5) that more clearly displays the problem over the past two weeks.

As the team turns its attention to Xui's quality assurance (QA) presentation, which shows failure by type (Figure 8.6), their understanding deepens.

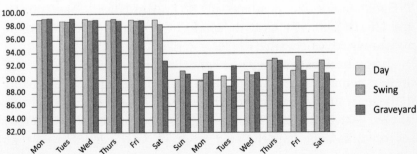

Yield at Final Test
(Previous Two Weeks)

FIGURE 8.5   Charting Yield at Final Test

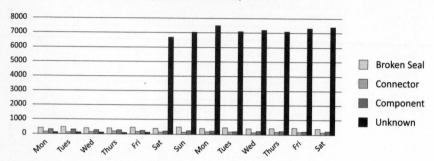

FIGURE **8.6** Chipset Failure Types

QA has not pinpointed the exact type of failure shared by the rejected chipsets. "This raises an interesting question," Xui suggests. "Did the chipsets actually fail final test, or is there a problem in the software?" The answer, she thinks, may lead the team to the root cause. First, however, they need to determine the type of failure, which to this point QA has been unable to diagnose. Now the team must pursue the identity of the real cause.

"Good news, bad news," Brad says. "The bad news is we don't know the type of failure. The good news is we know where to look for it. What do we need to do next? What will take us closer to understanding the problem? I propose we use a cause-and-effect diagram— you know, the old fishbone diagram—to brainstorm theories."

As shown in Figure 8.7, they begin by putting the undesired EFFECT in the box at the right, or "fishhead," and then adding "bones" behind the fishhead that detail possible causes of the EFFECT (under the headings PEOPLE, MACHINES, MATERIALS, and METHODS). The exercise sparks a lot of animated discussion, and a number of possible causes emerge.

Brad observes that they need to collect more data about some of these potential causes. Maria, the test engineer, agrees, suggesting the team restrict its search to whatever causes could have led to a sudden change in yield. Everyone agrees that makes sense, so they set to work developing the next round of data, using these if-then scenarios:

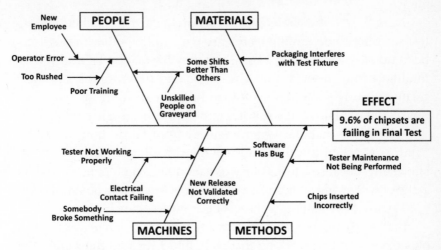

FIGURE **8.7** Matrix's Cause and Effect Diagram

- ◆ If it's an operator error, then we need to examine the *training and experience* of the graveyard employees.
- ◆ If the software contains faulty code, then we need to see *when it was released and/or updated.*
- ◆ If there's a problem with maintenance, then we need to know *when the tester last went through its preventative maintenance schedule.*
- ◆ If something extraordinary happened on that Saturday night, then we need to track down that *unusual event.*

Brad assigns tasks appropriate to the team members most familiar with those aspects of the process. Brad himself will visit with the Saturday evening crew in final test to see if any of them remember anything unusual happening that night. "Okay, gang, let's get to it. We'll meet back here at 4:00 PM." Again, that gives everyone sufficient time to conduct a thorough investigation.

At the 4:00 meeting, Billie Jo, the materials expeditor, takes the initiative. "I checked with personnel and discovered that three of the seven people working that night in final test were new recruits, with minimum training and no prior experience on the job. All three completed their training on Friday and went to work in final test for the first time on Saturday."

Next, Maria, the test engineer, reports that she checked into the test software to determine its release date and whether or not it had been updated since then. "Turns out they haven't had a new release in almost four months, but it was updated two months ago. So it seems unlikely some new software bug just showed up out of the blue," she explains. "It's not impossible, but it's highly unlikely."

Aditya, the manufacturing engineer from fabrication, raises her hand. "I checked out the tester maintenance log," she reports. "It's interesting, because it turns out *major* monthly maintenance was done at the end of swing shift on Saturday, just before our problem showed up. I suspect something went wrong in maintenance."

Brad nods agreement. "I reached five of the seven test associates, plus the supervisor working that shift, and I learned the same thing Billie Jo did. Almost half of the crew was brand new, which led to a good deal of normal first-day confusion. The supervisor had understandably accepted the sudden yield drop."

"So, this is all good input," concludes Brad. "Where do you guys think we ought to go next?"

David, from assembly, who had so far remained silently attentive throughout the discussion, suggests, "We need to pull someone in from maintenance and ask him or her to educate us about how they do their work. Something went wrong at shift-change, and unless we understand what they do and how they do it, we won't be able to get to the bottom of this. Shall I call my buddy Jason, who runs maintenance on the testers and ask him to join us first thing in the morning?"

"Great idea, David," says Aditya. "Then we can map the tester maintenance process and see if we can isolate where things went wrong."

Brad adjourns the second-day session with 24 hours left on the ticking clock.

At 8:00 AM the next morning Jason joins the team and summarizes the important steps in the maintenance process (see Figure 8.8). The team quickly draws a process map for it.

Jason tells them that in order to eliminate downtime, workers perform maintenance between shift changes. They order the necessary parts from materials (cleaning brushes, test contacts, and special cleaning pads to remove particles from the optical positioner). "It's a little tricky," he confesses. "We need to keep four different styles

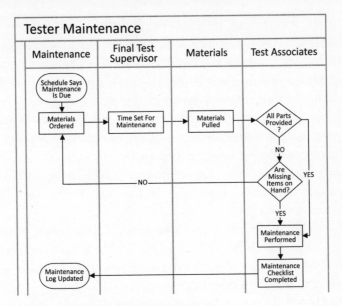

Tester Maintenance

Maintenance	Final Test Supervisor	Materials	Test Associates

Schedule Says Maintenance Is Due → Materials Ordered → Time Set For Maintenance → Materials Pulled → All Parts Provided? — NO → Are Missing Items on Hand? — YES → Maintenance Performed → Maintenance Checklist Completed → Maintenance Log Updated

FIGURE 8.8 Steps in the Maintenance Process

of test contacts on hand. Sometimes they break during production, and the test associates must replace them immediately. It's not unusual for the materials department to run out of certain contacts if the test associates have ordered a lot of them separately."

The map and Jason's added information help the team pinpoint the next round of data gathering. If the problem stems from an issue with the parts replaced during maintenance, they need to find out if any parts were missing during the problematic graveyard maintenance routine. Jason offers to make a quick call to answer that question.

"I have another suggestion," adds Billie Jo. "I think we ought to check to see if there were any new employees working in the department on the swing shift that night. Who knows, someone new might have helped with maintenance."

To allow Jason and Billie Jo time to get the relevant facts, Brad calls for a one-hour recess. He also asks Jason if he can bring samples of the maintenance parts to the meeting so the team can take a good look at them.

An hour later the team returns and picks up where they left off. The whole team is excited that they seem on the verge of uncovering the root cause of the problem. Jason leads off with a revealing bit of information. It turns out, he explains, that the maintenance parts kit used during the shift that Saturday night did not include one of the test contacts. He holds up three one-inch-wide discs of silvery metal with tiny copper bumps on their surface. "You'll remember that the kits usually contain four different styles of this little guy."

Billie Jo goes next. "I found out from HR that two brand-new employees were working in final test on swing," she reports. "That could have contributed to the problem."

Staring intently at the contact points, David shakes his head. "I can't see any difference. They all look the same to me. How do you know which one to use?"

"The training covers that," says Maria. "But the test software shouldn't have failed the chip just because of a bad contact point. Instead, it should have sent a contact error code indicating a bad connection to the tested device."

David holds up two of the contact points. "Could using the wrong contact cause a short, or something, that would fool test software?"

"I don't think so," says Maria.

Aditya stands up. "I have an idea. Why don't we walk over to the assembly plant and start poking around final test to see if somehow the contacts got mixed up?"

When they arrive at the final test station, the shift supervisor, Tom Howard, gives them a guided tour of the final test station. José, one of the test operators, takes his position at a waist-high console that looks like something from the flight deck of the Starship *Enterprise*. He explains that the automated unit tests 10 chipsets at a time. Aditya asks José to stop the tester for a minute and help Jason examine the contacts to see if the right contacts are in the right positions on the tester. José holds one up, exclaiming, "Got it! Wrong little guy in the wrong spot."

"Yay!" shouts Aditya. "This one fixture has the wrong contact. Folks, we have found the root cause of our problem!" Jason switches out the bad contact and releases the tester back into production.

Xui points out that several thousand presumably defective parts are sitting in a quality assurance bin, but that they may very well pass inspection with the test contact problem resolved.

While the team heads back across campus to its meeting room, Jason runs a couple hundred of the chipsets sitting in QA to check out Xui's theory.

One mystery remains, however: Why didn't the test software sound an alert about the contact problem?

"I have a theory about that," says Maria. "Let me run over and talk to the engineer responsible for that piece of software. I want him to check something. I'll catch up with you guys back in the meeting room."

Once everyone but Jason has settled into their chairs a half hour later, the team plunges into step 4.

Step 4: Develop Solutions

Consider alternative solutions and choose the best one. Assess its impact on surrounding processes. Complete an implementation workplan.

The project's sponsor, CEO Anita Houser, joins the team at this crucial stage. "I am hoping you guys have some good news," she says, a nervous smile revealing the stress that has been mounting for days.

Brad summarizes what Maria discovered when she chatted with the software engineer. Two months earlier, when a Matrix technician had validated new software, she had, as required, turned off a specific feature that validates a good connection between the tester and the chipset.

After validation, the new software went into service with that feature still disabled. That mistake, coupled with the insertion of the wrong contact point in the tester's number-seven position, accounted for the high failure rate. With the contact error element in the software turned on and the proper contact in place, the problem should disappear.

Just as Brad finishes the explanation, Jason walks into the room. "Well, I have good news," says Jason. "We just ran 200 of the thousands of chipsets parked in QA waiting for disposition because of this issue, and 199 of them passed with flying colors, our normal pass rate. There's nothing wrong with these sets after all."

After congratulations all around, Anita departs, and the team goes back to work, making sure their solutions will not adversely affect other processes. Quite often, especially in complicated systems, a change in one process will affect succeeding ones and cause more problems downstream. It takes little discussion for the team to conclude that, in this case, the only consequence downstream will be happy customers who will get their chipsets on time.

Step 5: Implement the Fix

Implement the solution. Monitor success and make any necessary adjustments.

The Matrix team orders the two solutions and hears from production that failure rates have indeed gone back to previous levels. They see no reason why they cannot keep hitting the target of .5 percent failure rates and on-time deliveries. Just to be safe, though, they agree that Brad will look at the numbers for every eight-hour shift for a full week. When the numbers remain steady, the team meets and agrees that the process will require no further adjustments at this time.

Step 6: Hold the Gain

Install a control that will prevent the root cause from reoccurring. Make sure any reoccurrence will receive immediate attention.

Controls come in variety of forms, including foolproofing (engineering a solution that makes it impossible for the error to reoccur), work aids that remind people how to implement it correctly, and process measures that turn yellow or red to signal the need for intervention.

The Matrix team chooses all three controls. First, they brainstorm ideas that would make it impossible for the tester contact error to occur in the future. Billie Jo suggests that the maintenance kits contain a *picture* of the fixture, showing exactly which part goes where. Xui adds that the kits could also include separate and clearly labeled plastic bags for each different contact point. Everyone agrees the combination of ideas would effectively reduce the chance for human error.

Aditya takes it a step further. "What if we modify the test fixture so only the right contact would fit in the right location? Given the tiny differences in their bases, I think we could do that quite easily."

The team agrees to move forward with all three ideas. Aditya promises to develop a workplan for modifying the test fixture.

With respect to the software glitch, Maria proposes another easy fix. "We can add a trigger to the code that will flash any disabled function on the screen, a warning that will not go away until someone turns it back on."

Finally, Brad recommends a process measure for final test with red/yellow/green ranges for levels of performance. Whenever performance slips into the yellow range, that signal will trigger an immediate call to action, instantly relaunching the problem-solving process.

A few weeks later, after Matrix has implemented all of the controls, the team can sit back and reflect on what it has accomplished.

Step 7: Reflect and Learn

Discuss the knowledge gained from the problem-solving experience. Document lessons learned for other problem solvers in the organization.

Anita and Brad facilitate a concluding session during which they talk about the experience. Did everyone enjoy working on the project? Did everyone feel satisfied with the results? Does anyone see a way to improve the process the next time around? Anita writes a one-page summary she can share with the leaders of future problem-solving teams. The summary emphasizes gathering *all* facts before jumping to a conclusion, making sure the team includes all relevant members (Jason joined the team midstream), and actually seeing the problem taking place (the team's visit to the shop floor). The best suggestion, she thinks, is to create a list of the nine most common mistakes problem solvers make. Teams could review that list at the beginning of every problem-solving project.

Nine Most Common Mistakes Problem Solvers Make

1. *Failing to follow the Seven Rules of Total Transparency.* Create a safe environment that banishes fear.
2. *Proceeding without a clear and specific charter.* If you don't know where you're going, that's where you'll end up.
3. *Looking for someone to blame.* Point your finger at the problem, not the person.
4. *Drawing conclusions before all the facts are on the table.* Solutions based on half-truths will solve half the problem half the time.
5. *Letting emotions flare.* Anger is part of the problem, not part of the solution.
6. *Getting personal.* Leave prejudice, judgment, and stereotypes at the door.
7. *Neglecting to install a control.* If you do not secure the boulder after you have pushed it to the top of the hill, it will go rolling back down and crush you.
8. *Oversolving a problem.* Concentrate on the task at hand, and do not allow secondary problems that pop up along the way to distract you.
9. *Failing to consider all input, no matter how crazy it sounds.* Sometimes, the best solutions come from "outside the box."

The case study in this chapter showed the application of a problem-solving discipline to a somewhat complex problem, yet the same skills, tools, and concepts apply to each and every NOW problem (remember, "problem" also means "opportunity"). As your employees become increasingly capable with problem solving, they will grow more and more comfortable with relying on facts, thinking through the implications of decisions, working collaboratively and transparently with others, and implementing speedy and effective solutions.

The NOW organization places effective problem-solving tools in the hands of each and every employee. Nothing contributes more to success in this Era of Mass Customization.

■　■　■

Complete the Speedometer for Solving Problems Now in Table 8.3 and add your net score to the summary sheet in the Appendix.

TABLE **8.3**　NOW Speedometer for Solving Problems Now

Then	−1	0	+1	Now
We do not use a common problem-solving method				We use a common problem-solving method
We do not stress transparency in the problem-solving process				We stress transparency in the problem-solving process
We do not train everyone to solve problems				We train everyone to solve problems
We emphasize complete creative freedom when solving problems				We emphasize creativity within a defined problem-solving methodology
We look for the people who caused the problem				We do not blame people for causing problems
We rely on a handful of problem solvers				We rely on everyone to solve problems
We often find the same problems recurring again and again				We install controls to make sure problems do not recur
Subtotals				
Solving Problems Now NET SCORE				

Add this score to the consolidated score in the Appendix.

Enabling the NOW Workforce

Banish Fear, Build Trust

U.S. Air Force E-4 Clint Thornton remained cool under fire as 500 rounds of 14.5 mm antiaircraft munitions lit up the night sky. Charged with taking possession of the bombed-out Al Asad Airbase, headquarters for the Iraqi Air Force, during the Operation Iraqi Freedom invasion in 2003, Clint watched calmly from his position overlooking the base. As the squad below began pursuing looters, the enemy's antiaircraft fire signaled the moment of truth for the 22-year-old. Calling on his three years of state-of-the-art training, he instantly began doing his job.

With men on the ground and jets poised overhead to attack the antiaircraft gun, Clint's job required a deft balancing act. After radioing a warning to the Australian Special Air Service squadron on the ground, Clint determined precise coordinates with his GPS satellite-connected range finder, contacted the pilots of two F/A-18 fighter jets overhead, and began directing them to the target. Seconds away from telling the pilots to bomb the target, Clint listened as one of the ground troops reported a figure running away from the weapon. In a split second, Clint decided to hold fire. The ground squad could take care of the situation.

"The first time you do it in training, you are scared out of your mind, because you don't want to make a mistake," Clint said later. "It's the training that gets you ready. In the training we used real bombs. They get you close to the experience, so you can actually feel it."

Rigorous close-air support training sessions had prepared Clint for his work, so that when the moment of truth arrived, he could instantly make the right decision. With lives on the line, his training banished fear and empowered him to do his job with distinction. Many people see the military as the model of command and control, but in reality front-line combat requires quick and accurate decision making.

Clint Thornton's training in the now gave him the competence, confidence, and security he needed to do his job at the speed of now:

- ◆ Excellent education (three years of intensive, multiple-scenario exercises)
- ◆ Clear rules (the U.S. military's "rules of engagement" for Iraq, which Clint committed to memory)
- ◆ Full permission (prior to the operation, the Australian regiment commander gave Clint the authority to take charge should air cover be required)
- ◆ Total support (Clint knew he could trust his commanding officer to back his decisions)

Soon after the Al Asad incident, Clint's preparation again came into play, when he and two fellow combat controllers and the Australian squadron repaired one of the bombed-out runways and set up landing lights in order to get one of the airport's landing strips back up and running. Although not ordered or authorized to do that work, the team took the initiative. Its prompt action led to the facility becoming the second-largest U.S. airbase in Iraq, and an invaluable conduit for sorely needed resources to the battlefield. For their efforts during the invasion, Clint and his U.S. peers won the Bronze Star for meritorious service.

Business today requires the same sort of decisiveness and initiative on the front lines.

People Want to Do the Right Thing

Consider the case of "SouthPac Trading." Middle manager "Valerie Simpson" needed a routine nondisclosure agreement to close an important deal with a new customer. Unable to reach her boss, who was en route to Asia and could not be reached for hours, Valerie contacted the administrative assistant to the company's legal counsel. "I need this now," she told the assistant, without explaining that a whopping $10-million-a-quarter contract depended on swift action.

At the other end of the line the assistant put Valerie on hold and rang her boss, who told her he could not take time just then for such a trivial matter, especially for someone he did not know personally. "Tell her I'll get to it when I get to it."

Valerie soon caught up with her own boss, "Ronald Feuerstein," and brought him up to speed on the deal. Ronald assured her legal would promptly take care of the matter. Early the next morning she anxiously phoned the administrative assistant in legal to ask when she could expect the necessary document. "We're dead in the water without it," she explained.

"I told him you needed it," the timid voice from the other end of the line murmured. "I think he'll get to it soon."

Fearful of the worst, Valerie called Ronald to update him on the situation.

Ronald reassured her. "He's a busy guy, Val. Not to worry, though, I'll be back in the office tomorrow morning. I'll make sure you get it."

When the day passed with no nondisclosure agreement, Valerie grew frantic, but she decided to soldier on and wait for Ronald's return. Sure enough, at 9:30 the next morning her boss showed up with the agreement in hand. "No big deal; he just fished the boilerplate out of his files, but he reminded me that such requests must come from vice presidents."

Valerie closed her eyes and took a deep breath. "Well, we lost the deal. That little piece of boilerplate cost us $40 million in gross margin, minimum."

Within months Valerie left the firm for a less stressful and more rewarding position. Good for her, you might say. Not so good for her former employer. Think about the millions of other Valeries, who also vote with their feet, leaving jobs because they refuse to tolerate bad "business as usual." According to Dr. Jessica Tracy, an associate professor of psychology at the University of British Columbia, human beings take "authentic pride" (as opposed to narcissistic pride) in doing a good job; but when performing challenging work, they need to feel they have significant control over the work itself.

"Pride is the emotional mechanism that allows people to have self-esteem," explains Dr. Tracy. "The ultimate function of pride is all about group inclusion and the sense of respect and high status with others."

In her research Dr. Tracy has discovered that authentic pride plays a major role in all aspects of our lives. Pride is correlated to lower levels of anxiety, depression, hostility, and aggression, and results in improved social behavior, better interpersonal relationships, and higher levels of agreeableness. It also makes people more conscientious.

Sadly, many people trade their pride for a paycheck, health insurance benefits, and, if they are lucky, a decent 401k plan with employer-matched contributions. When they make that trade-off, they may soon find their work so dehumanizing they start leaving their brains at home. Almost anyone who has worked in multiple organizations has had this experience, or at least has seen it happen to others. Good people start out wanting to do the right thing, but when they find their efforts consistently blocked by "the way we do things around here," they give up.

It is easy to draw the conclusion that employees are lazy or don't care about doing a good job. In fact, behind these behaviors are usually understandable reasons why people resort to these coping strategies (listed in Table 9.1). It boils down to simple pain avoidance. When efforts to fix something are repeatedly blocked, people will begin to protect themselves from further disappointment by avoiding responsibility or shifting the blame. The bottom line may seem counterintuitive, but to change that type of behavior you must respond with *less* management control, not more.

Fear Blocks Initiative

Fear struck the heart of a small community-based newspaper in the Northwest after "Fred Simmons," the publisher of "Comm News Corp" (CNC) gathered his staff to issue his usual threat. "If I didn't believe in CNC's mission, I'd shut it down. We cannot keep on hemorrhaging money. You guys have got to get into high gear."

TABLE **9.1** Employee Coping Strategies

Strategy	Coping Rationale
Go along to get along	I must hold back opinions, to avoid potential disagreement, and for fear of earning a reputation as a troublemaker, someone who just doesn't fit in.
Blame others for mistakes	I must deflect blame when things go wrong, to avoid criticism or punishment.
Duck new assignments	I must avoid involvement in a new project for fear it will turn out badly.
Delay decisions	I must distance myself from making a decision, to avoid criticism for a poor one.
Follow orders blindly	I must do only what a superior tells me to do.
Adhere to "That's the way we do things around here"	I must not say or do anything that runs counter to the status quo.

Although none of Fred's small staff had worked for the regional chain of small newspapers for more than a year, they knew that the problem did not stem from their laziness. No, the root cause of company's troubles was sagging advertising revenues, caused by the vacancy created when CNC's only ad sales rep quit four months earlier. Why had this vital position gone unfilled so long? Perhaps candidates for the job knew Fred's reputation as an overbearing boss.

"Jona Bright," the 25-year-old editor who routinely put in a 60-hour week, watched Fred wrap up the meeting and walk out the door. "How can he hold us all responsible for something *he's* failed to do?" she wondered out loud to her colleagues. "We've turned this paper around. Readership is up 15 percent. He's not doing *his* job, yet he's blaming *us* for the problem? Give me a break."

Not surprisingly, Fred felt betrayed a week later when Jona handed him her resignation, saying she'd landed another job with a fast-growing online news source compiler.

As a manager, Fred would fail the final exam in Human Motivation 101. The moment he steps foot in the door, his staff dreads their interactions with him. His behavior, more than the current precariousness of the newspaper business, is what accounted for the high turnover at CNC. No wonder the company keeps bleeding red ink.

While Fred may exhibit a rather extreme case of "management by scare tactics," he's not alone in the world of *motivational malpractice*. Many managers, wielding power over the fate of their employees, create an environment where people grow afraid to say what they really think. Worse, they say what they *think* the boss wants to hear. Ironically, a manager's own fear often motivates the use of scare tactics. Look into the heart of any playground bully, and you'll find a scared little kid who fears looking weak or powerless.

Why did Clint Thornton do such a great job on the battlefield? His superiors, both during training and at the beginning of deployment, banished the fear that generates failure. The same applies to doing *business at the speed of now*. Frightened people either avoid making decisions, or make bad ones. Confident, well-trained people welcome the moment of truth and act promptly and effectively the instant it arrives.

When psychologist Abraham Maslow proposed a hierarchy of needs to explain human behavior, he ranked the need for "safety" second on the list (see Figure 9.1). This human need plays itself out in the workplace when an employee's desire to speak the truth meets

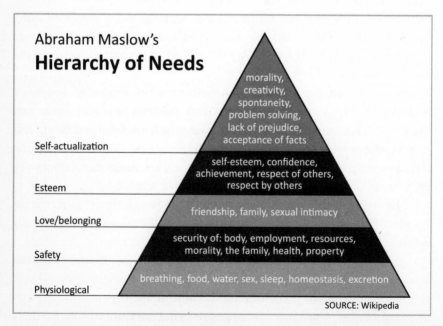

FIGURE 9.1   Maslow's Hierarchy of Needs

the fear of a public reprimand or even dismissal. When saying or doing something might threaten your livelihood and security, you will do whatever it takes to protect yourself.

Many different fears can jeopardize your sense of safety at work, from the fear of saying something that may label you a troublemaker to the fear of doing something wrong that will find its way onto your performance review. Such worries can even affect your health, as you spend most of your time in a state of mental distress. Fear can also become a self-fulfilling prophecy. When people fear losing their job, they can easily freeze whenever they need to make a decision, thus further contributing to declining performance and eventual job loss.

Getting labeled as a troublemaker or a marginal performer damages a person's self esteem, another level in Maslow's hierarchy. If you work in an organization that punishes you for speaking your mind or challenging the status quo, any attempt to do so will win you a reputation as a malcontent, a squeaky wheel, and a poor team player. The converse holds true: If you work for an organization that encourages truth-telling and new ideas that challenge the status quo, doing so makes you part of the successful crowd. Sadly, the former mind-set dominates most traditional organizations today.

Building a Foundation for Trust

Martin Luther King said something truly insightful in an interview in March of 1957: "Whenever you have a transition, whenever you are moving from one system to another, there will be definite difficulties, but I think there is enough brainpower, and I think there is enough determination, enough courage and faith to meet the difficulties as they develop. I often feel like saying, when I hear the question 'People aren't ready,' that it's like telling a person who is trying to swim, 'Don't jump in that water until you learn how to swim,' when actually you will never learn how to swim until you get in the water." King believed that people craved the opportunity to develop and govern themselves.

When managers in THEN organizations encourage the coping strategies that give people a false sense of security, they prevent them from "jumping into the water." Consequently, they stall the transition to a new and better NOW system. Does this mean that managers should give their people unrestricted freedom? No. Freedom unbalanced by responsibility and order results in anarchy; and anarchy thwarts progress and productivity just as much as strict command and control. The participative management/self-directed work teams movement of the 1980s, sparked by such books as William Ouchi's *Theory Z: How American Management Can Meet the Japanese Challenge,* fell short of expectations because that approach bestowed freedom without respecting the complexity of human beings and the realities of what organizations need to accomplish to remain viable. When it comes to making the transition from *then* to *now,* people can't just suddenly dive into a formless void that may or may not contain any water. They need a pool whose bottom they can see and a clear sense of what they must accomplish when they dive into it.

Freedom thrives on a foundation of order. No nation prospers without the order created by law. The founding fathers of the United States understood that while people wanted the freedom to live productive lives and pursue happiness, they needed to do so within a prescribed order that made sense to them. As they fashioned the Constitution, they struggled to articulate the right balance. After much debate, they came down on the side of more freedom than order. Each organization must establish a set point that best suits its circumstances. Some, such as a military unit, might require more order; others, such as a design studio, may require less. Regardless of your own set point, once you establish it, you begin building trust (see Figure 9.2).

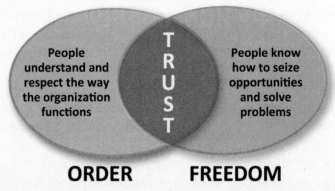

FIGURE **9.2** Balancing Order and Freedom to Build Trust

Too much on either side of the scale can lead to ruin. Heavy-handed order engenders revolt by people who feel oppressed; unbridled freedom breeds chaos. The equation applies to all organizations, both public and private. Human beings will trade freedom for order if that will give them the most benefits. But if the order becomes excessive, they will revolt and press for freedom.

To move to the now, order must precede freedom, because order defines the boundaries in which the freedom can flourish. Chapters 5 through 8 of this book defined the order needed to provide a viable foundation for the now.

Helping People Cross the Divide

You can also think about this equation as a sort of continental divide, with dictatorial order on one side (then) and order-based freedom (now) on the other. People naturally want to cross the divide by improving their lot in life and doing the right thing. To make that journey, they need to feel safe. They need to trust those who have established the order. Dictators do not make people feel safe, nor do leaders who never set boundaries and let chaos and confusion reign. In order for managers to help people make the transition from *then* to *now*, they must convince them that they themselves are committed to the change and that they will do everything in their power to help everyone complete the journey successfully.

I learned this lesson in the late 1980s when I ran the manufacturing department for Floating Point Systems. We had recently instituted a major change in pay structures, reducing the number of job classifications from 19 to 6 and setting up a pay-for-knowledge system that rewarded people for learning new skills. This would, we thought, inspire people to grow and become more versatile and valuable to the company.

Soon after we completed the initiative, two Laotian employees, "Dao" and "Kham," asked to meet with their "Big Boss," as they called me. Dao, a grandmotherly woman who worked in circuit board assembly, spoke for them both.

"Good morning," she said. " We came to see you because Kham's pay is not right with the change you just made. She has the same skills as me and should be paid the same."

Her much younger companion nodded her assent.

Dao's words stunned me, not because of what she said but because she had said anything at all.

The plant employed a large number of Southeast Asian men and women, many of whom had fled to the United States during the Vietnam War era. They brought with them a tradition that dictated respectful subservience to the boss, especially from women. That, coupled with their weak grasp of the English language, kept them quiet, even when they saw a problem or felt badly treated.

To remedy that situation and help our Southeast Asian employees become more valuable members of the Floating Point family, we had introduced English language and culture classes one hour per week, half held during lunch breaks, half on company time. Dao and Kham had faithfully attended those classes.

Dao's words made a big impression on me. Here was a woman who had crossed the divide. Once fearful and subservient and silent, she now felt safe to speak up when she saw an injustice caused by our new pay system. Now, she trusted the company, and she trusted me. I thanked both women profusely and promised to fix the problem that very day.

Trust and training builds confidence. They built it for Dao and Kham, and they built it for Clint Thornton. As you shift your management system from *then* to *now*, you should monitor the levels of safety and trust and confidence your people feel when they encounter both opportunities and problems. Without a sense of safety, no one will voice their concerns. Without the right skills, they will not voice the right concerns.

Recall the conditions that made Clint Thornton so effective. The first two establish order; the last two bestow freedom.

◆ Excellent education
◆ Clear rules
◆ Full permission
◆ Total support

As we just explored, crossing over from then to the now demands a balance between order and freedom, a balance that forms the

You might take a few moments here to go back and review the Seven Deadly Sins of Management (Chapter 2) and the Three NOW Gears (Chapter 3) and the ways by which you can eliminate fear, reduce variation, and pursue constraints. Remind yourself, too, of the NOW Mindset you want every member of your workforce to adopt (i.e., I use facts to find truth, I serve my customers, I improve my processes, I know that people count on me, I keep score to maintain focus).

Consider, too, the skills your people need to solve problems quickly and effectively. Reflect on the way scorecards related to routine work and Quarterly Target Reviews reinforce the need to seize opportunities and solve problems. Chapters 5 through 8 help you establish the order it takes to manage a company successfully in the now. That order includes every employee understanding the organization's direction, their role, how they take accountability for results, and how they solve problems.

foundation for trust. Use the Trust Checklist in Figure 9.3, which encompasses seven key elements that balance order and freedom, to help you achieve this important goal.

TRUST CHECKLIST

ORDER			FREEDOM
Clear vision/goals			To contribute
Line of sight to my role			To do the right thing
Full accountability			To measure performance
Shared business language			To speak freely
Maximum transparency			To feel safe
Resources to do the job			To access needed information
Tools/skills to be effective			To achieve peak performance

FIGURE 9.3 Trust Checklist

1. *A clear vision and goals free people to contribute.* People love to do challenging work that makes a difference, accomplishing something that gives them a strong sense that they are contributing not only to their own welfare but also to the welfare of others.

2. *A clear line of sight to their roles and accountabilities frees people to do the right thing.* People need to see how their work connects to the overall organization. They desire control over their work and need the authority to fix the problems they encounter.

3. *Full accountability frees people to measure their performance.* People will not feel comfortable taking accountability for results if they cannot measure their own performance.

4. *A shared business language frees people to speak freely.* People can more quickly and effectively seize opportunities, solve problems, and implement their ideas when they speak the same language. A commonly understood language also encourages them to talk about their concerns.

5. *Maximum transparency frees people to feel safe.* People need to feel free to act, with the knowledge that everyone makes mistakes when solving problems and that they will not be punished for honest errors. People learn as much from their mistakes as from their successes.

6. *Resources to do the job frees people to access the information they need.* People cannot do their work at the speed of now unless they can access the information they need to make quick and effective decisions. Cloud computing and social media help them do that. People also need a skilled coach or mentor to provide support and guidance.

7. *Tools/skills to be effective free people to achieve peak performance.* People need the right skills and tools to do their jobs well. In the NOW organization, this includes not only job-specific training but training in the use of social media and cloud computing.

The millennial mind-set demands an environment of trust. Technological tools such as social media and cloud computing can do a lot to help create it. Such an environment also depends on managers shifting their thinking from permitting people to get results to expecting them to do so.

Shifting from Permit to Expect

Gary Convis, former president of Toyota in Georgetown, Kentucky, describes Toyota's expectations of its employees simply: "Only two things: come to work and pull the cord."

Toyota, famous for the fact that any employee can stop the production line by tugging on a cord, has long understood that managers must give their people full authority to stop the process and solve problems the moment they occur. Managers at the company trust their people and give them the freedom to act. As a result, workers view the person who receives their work as their customer, and will not knowingly ship a known defect down the line. They do the right thing, with confidence. They do not fear taking action, and they do not need to get permission to take it; they do so because managers expect nothing less from them.

Toyota has struck the right balance between order and freedom. People are trained to do their jobs, they know how their jobs fit into the larger picture, and they react quickly when the need arises. They do *business at the speed of now* inside the organization. This contrasts sharply with the *then* practice of spotting a defective part, laying it aside, and hoping the next part will pass inspection. Meanwhile, the defective part goes to the quality department because quality is not the assembly-line worker's problem. If the worker receives another defective part, the process repeats itself, ad infinitum.

Like any company, however, Toyota can get into trouble when doing the right thing fails to permeate every process, as happened during the company's massive auto and truck recalls of 2010 and 2011, due to faulty floor mats that caused accidental acceleration. This defect occurred because the company's emphasis on swift problem solving on the front lines did not find its way to distribution and service affiliates. The affiliates should have seen the floor mat problem emerging, and intervened early to correct it, *before* it escalated into a full-blown safety and public relations disaster.

The shift from permitting people to do the right thing to expecting them to do it marks an important shift in management thinking,

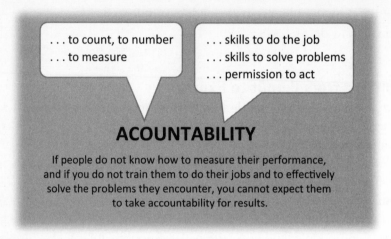

... to count, to number
... to measure

... skills to do the job
... skills to solve problems
... permission to act

ACOUNTABILITY

If people do not know how to measure their performance,
and if you do not train them to do their jobs and to effectively
solve the problems they encounter, you cannot expect them
to take accountability for results.

FIGURE **9.4**   Components of Accountability

because it replaces the THEN idea of "doing the work" to the NOW idea of "improving how the work gets done." In Toyota's case, it explains why the plant in Georgetown, Kentucky, implements 90,000 employee ideas per year.

This same shift in thinking also raises the issue of accountability. What does *accountability* really mean? The widely recognized experts on accountability, Roger Connors and Tom Smith, authors of *The Oz Principle: Getting results Through Individual and Organizational Accountability* means that people see, own, and act to solve problems. It's all about getting results, "counting" results, and gaining the "ability" to do the work (see Figure 9.4).

If you make sure people know what you expect, if you train them to perform effectively, and if you show them how to measure performance against expectations, then you have implemented accountability in your organization.

The shift from giving people permission to perform and expecting them to get results moves through predictable stages we call the Seven Stages of YESability, shown in Figure 9.5 and defined further here:

Stage 1: Follow orders. Managers tell employees what to do and do not tolerate any form of insubordination.

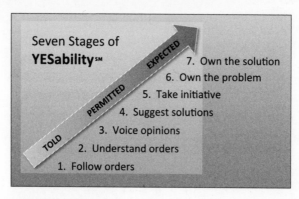

Figure 9.5 YESability Stages

Stage 2: Understand orders. Managers tell employees *why* they should follow orders.

Stage 3: Voice opinions. Managers encourage employees to speak up and share their thoughts and opinions.

Stage 4: Suggest solutions. Managers welcome employee ideas about solving problems.

Stage 5: Take initiative. Managers encourage employees to take the initiative to solve problems.

Stage 6: Own the problem. Managers give employees the authority to take action, and the tools they need to do so, promptly and effectively.

Stage 7: Own the solution. Managers make it clear that they expect every employee to seize every opportunity every time.

Once you have fully progressed from permit to expect, YESability will begin to permeate your entire organization.

Any great organization is greater than the sum of the people who work in it. Freedom for each individual to act quickly and effectively to ensure personal and collective success creates a dynamic environment, where people accomplish more than they dreamed possible.

As you work to banish fear and build trust in your own organization, you will wrestle with some of the most important and difficult decisions you'll ever make. Striking the right balance of order and freedom will take a lot of careful thought in the beginning, followed by

constant vigilance in the years ahead. How would you rate your
organization right now?

■ ■ ■

Complete the Speedometer for Enabling the NOW Workforce in
Table 9.2 and add your net score to the summary sheet in the Appendix.

TABLE **9.2**   NOW Speedometer 9: Enabling the NOW Workforce

Then	–1	0	+1	Now
We provide basic training				We provide extensive and ongoing training
We fear problems				We tackle problems without fear of making mistakes
We do not feel confident about reaching our objectives				We feel extremely confident that we will reach our objectives
We avoid taking initiative because we may get in trouble				We work in an environment where no one gets punished for an honest mistake
We don't establish complete and clear expectations for results				We establish complete and clear expectations for results
We do not feel safe to take action				We feel completely safe to take swift action
We must seek permission to seize opportunities and to solve problems				We expect everyone to seize every opportunity and solve every problem every time
Subtotals				

The NOW Workforce **NET SCORE** [　]

Add this score to the consolidated score in the Appendix.

SPEEDOMETER

THEN		NOW
-7 -6 -5 -4 -3 -2 -1	0	+1 +2 +3 +4 +5 +6 +7

Becoming a NOW Leader

Stop Bossing, Start Teaching

"Technology served as an accelerant," said Alec Ross, U.S. Secretary of State Hillary Clinton's senior adviser for innovation, about the 2011 overthrow of Hosni Mubarak's government in Egypt. "A movement that historically would have taken months or years was compressed into far shorter time cycles."

Historically, revolutions usually required a charismatic leader and took a long time to unfold. It took years for change to sweep through Elizabethan England, Cuba, and the United States under the guiding hands of Oliver Cromwell, Fidel Castro, and George Washington, respectively. Nowadays, however, a revolution can start with a 140-character tweet from a nameless, faceless revolutionary, and it can succeed in mere hours or days. In the case of the overthrow of Mubarak, no single compelling figure emerged to lead the charge, yet it took mere weeks for the three-decades-old Mubarak dictatorship to go down in flames. Social media struck the match.

"Without Facebook, without Twitter, without Google, without YouTube, this would have never happened," Wael Ghonim told CBS correspondent Harry Smith on *60 Minutes*. Ghonim, the Google executive and behind-the-scenes cyberactivist who helped propel the movement, had launched the "We are all Khaled Saeed"

Facebook page to tell the story of a young Egyptian businessman who had been beaten to death by the Egyptian police. The page quickly attracted 400,000 followers, creating a virtual revolutionary meeting hall where disaffected Egyptians could gather, communicate, and organize. The page called for the January 25, 2011, protest that drew hundreds of thousands of protestors into the nation's streets, all clamoring for the ouster of the powerful and corrupt government. It all happened because social media united people from diverse social, political, and economic backgrounds and interests into a massive, unstoppable force.

By definition, leaders need followers. But in the case of the Egyptian revolt, and other widespread phenomena driven by social media, change can come from the bottom up rather than from the top down. In a NOW world, leaders must understand and harness the power of this new reality. Those who try to fight it could easily follow Hosni Mubarak into exile.

Thousands of theories have come along about the best way to manage and lead people, and it would take a whole book to explore all the beliefs and tools effective leaders use to help their people do *business at the speed of now*. This chapter will concentrate on the most important one: shifting from boss to teacher. That shift includes moving:

1. *From no to yes.* Replace preventing people from doing the wrong thing to helping them figure out for themselves how to do the right thing.
2. *From disconnection to full engagement.* Replace the assumption that people have connected to the organization's mission to helping them fully engage in achieving it.
3. *From know-it-all to fellow learner.* Replace acting like the fount of all knowledge and wisdom to acting like a student yourself.
4. *From frozen layer to fear defroster.* Replace obstructing people from thinking for themselves to encouraging them to make their own sound decisions.
5. *From commander to inspirational guide.* Replace telling people what to do with inspiring them to participate in a great achievement.

From No to Yes

Speaking before a new group of "Sequoia Computer" line workers during their initial orientation meeting, President and CEO "Steve Workman" said, "See the red light here on our manufacturing line? If anyone—and I mean *anyone, anywhere, anytime*—sees *anything* wrong, you must step up and turn on that light. We will stop the line immediately. And it will stay stopped until we've solved the problem."

That was rule number one.

Just as Steve was about to move on to rule number two, new recruit "Mary White" ran over and turned on the light, bringing the line to an abrupt halt.

Steve, glaring at her in disbelief, demanded, "Why did you do that?"

"I saw an error in the instructions for one of the boards I will be building."

"You saw an error? You haven't even started work on the line yet. How could you see an error?"

"Right here, on page three," she said. "It reads 'circiut' instead of 'circuit.'"

Steve, rolling his eyes, said, "But that is not the kind of problem I'm talking about."

Mary stood her ground. "You said *anyone, anywhere, anytime*; if we see *anything* wrong!"

Obviously, Mary interpreted the rule too literally. Steve had, in fact, told the new troops exactly what to do—but he neglected to add that they should use their own good judgment before turning on the emergency light. Like many leaders, Steve wanted to make the rules perfectly clear, but he had failed to explain that the rules had certain boundaries, wherein people could and should think for themselves. He was saying no to any exceptions to the rule, when he should have been saying yes to individual initiative.

Replacing no with yes does not mean that from now on you give everyone permission to do whatever they want. You draw clear boundaries to establish order, and you provide language and methods people can use to solve problems. You become an enabler of action rather than an unwitting obstacle to performance.

In the Then world of command and control, "no" dominates a manager's vocabulary. But it's not just the word; it's the action. Closing

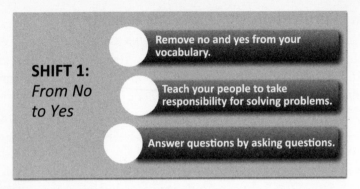

FIGURE **10.1** From No to Yes

doors to avoid interruptions, demanding that people "put it in writing," using accountability as a tool for punishment, employing body language that tells people "Don't bother me unless it's an emergency," and displaying a demeanor that suggests you do not suffer fools gladly all say no as loudly as if it you had spoken the word.

In a NOW world, yes replaces no in a manager's vocabulary (see Figure 10.1). "What do *you* think about this issue?" "How would you suggest we solve this problem?" You also say yes when you remove your door from its hinges, literally or figuratively. You say yes when you listen with an open mind, when you use accountability as a motivational tool, when you encourage informal interactions with your people, when you let people know you think there's no such thing as a stupid idea, and when you send all the other nonverbal signals that speak yes as if it had come from your lips.

Words and actions teach. They show instead of tell. They replace a preordained answer with a guiding hand.

1. *Remove no and yes from your vocabulary.* Few business problems lend themselves to easy black or white solutions. If mailroom clerk Gareth comes to you for a decision about whether or not to absorb the additional cost of shipping an order overnight to an important customer, don't just state the company policy, help him explore the gray areas where the company should make an exception to that policy.
2. *Teach your people to take responsibility for solving problems.* When people seek a yes/no answer, they basically shift the

responsibility for the outcome to someone else. If you tell Gareth, "No, we do not pay for overnight shipping on such a small order," then he ducks responsibility when the important customer demands to know why he didn't make an exception in this case.

3. *Answer questions by asking questions.* When people ask you questions, ask them questions in return. Answering their question robs them of an opportunity to think for themselves. Rather than stating the company policy when Gareth asks, "Should we absorb the extra cost of overnight shipping?" ask, "What do you think?" Gareth may decide for himself whether or not the order is large enough or the customer important enough to make an exception in this case.

From Disconnection to Full Engagement

"Every night when I was leaving my office as secretary of state," recalls retired General Colin Powell, "I would see the man coming in who cleaned my office. I would always make it a point to thank him. He needed to understand that if my office looked good, it reflected well on the United States. He needed to understand he played a key role."

Powell consistently acknowledged well-done work and built pride through phone calls to spouses and handwritten notes to the people who worked for him. "It isn't hard to turn people on," said the former chairman of the Joint Chiefs of Staff. It may not be hard, but a lot of managers act as if such gestures are beneath them.

As emphasized in Chapter 9, pride comes not just from accomplishing a challenging task but also from knowing you exercised a great deal of control over the outcome. When you take full control of the outcome, you put yourself on the line, and that can be scary, but not as scary as loss of control. The change roller coaster may be flying along the rails at breakneck speed, but it's always better to grip the controls than to let go, sit back, and pray you won't crash and burn. To conquer fear and build pride, you must shift people from disconnection to full engagement. You must drive home the organization's greater purpose, the role each worker plays in fulfilling the purpose, and acknowledge that the journey will get scary at times (see Figure 10.2).

Figure 10.2   From Fear to Pride

Here are three actions you can take to make the shift from disconnection to full engagement, and how to take them:

1. *Connect people to something that really matters.* People want to make a difference by participating in an important cause. When people can see how their work contributes to the cause, their efforts take on purpose and meaning. Show people that the day-to-day job of laying bricks is not "bricklaying" but "building a cathedral."

2. *Issue an exciting challenge.* Authentic pride comes from challenging work. Challenge people and help them get excited about seizing opportunities and solving problems. "If we can get the spire on top three months ahead of the original schedule, it will be ready for the millennial celebration."

3. *Acknowledge fear of change.* Doing the job better and doing it faster requires change, and change instills fear. Acknowledge that fact and promise to help people conquer their fear. "I know it seems impossible to finish this cathedral sooner than planned, and that scares me, too; but if we all put our best effort into the job, we will get it done in time for the millennial celebration."

From Know-It-All to Fellow Learner

"When I got back from vacation I discovered there had been a revolt," confides James Schroeder, now CEO of Care Oregon Community Health, a not-for-profit start-up serving the healthcare needs of people who can't afford mainstream care. He was talking about the time when, at the tender age of 25, he had been managing his first clinic. He had returned from a much-needed vacation to learn from his boss that 75 percent of this 30-person operation had come to her saying that either she fire Schroeder or they would quit.

Reflecting back on that time, he admits, "I was younger than most of the people, and I figured I had to prove my worth by showing them how much I knew."

As it turned out, Schroeder's boss backed him, not because she believed he was 100 percent right but because she did not think the employee threat of quitting was an appropriate way to express their dissatisfaction.

"I was so out of touch that I had no idea people were so unhappy," recalls Schroeder. "I learned you can get a lot more accomplished working *with* people rather than trying to get them to work *for* you."

In a NOW organization, everyone learns and everyone teaches. Both teachers and students maintain humility because humility lays common ground (see Figure 10.3). Teachers make mistakes, and when they do, they must admit it. If they forget their new role in the now, and return to bossing people around, they should admit that, too. An apology will go a long way toward setting things right with people, who will certainly forgive an honest mistake and understand backsliding.

1. *Stress that everyone should learn something new every day.* Watch for opportunities to level the playing field by telling your

FIGURE **10.3**   From Know-It-All to Fellow Learner

employees you don't know any more than they do about the work. Ask for advice. When Barbara presents a puzzling problem with a software update, admit that you need to learn about it, too. Ask her, "When you figure this out, will you teach me and the rest of the team what to do about it?"

2. *Apologize when you act as if you know all the answers.* You will make your fair share of mistakes, and you will probably slip back into the old bossy mode. When you do, try to catch yourself immediately and apologize for your error. "I'm sorry I told you I'd get an answer for you, Barbara. I should have given you the green light to go ahead and look for good solutions on your own. You know more about the new software than anyone, and solving this problem will help out the whole team."

3. *Admit your vulnerability.* Old-fashioned bosses will often try to bluff their way through a challenging situation because they fear that admitting their fallibility will make them look weak. Nothing could be further from the truth. Peoples' hearts go out to colleagues who admit their vulnerability. "Barbara, I'm not fully up to speed on the technical details of the new software. I'm relying on you to figure it out and help me get a handle on it."

From Frozen Layer to Fear Defroster

I recall the time I ran an assembly department in a company that could not avoid a layoff. Quite a few people were going to lose their jobs during a big slump in the midrange-class supercomputer market. Everyone knew the layoffs were coming and, in particular, that the circuit board assembly department would take a serious hit. One of the best assemblers, an employee named Dan, came to me as the designated spokesperson for the 35-member assembly workforce. He said that the group had decided they wanted me to sit down with the whole team to announce the specific layoffs. They knew that about half of them would leave the meeting with pink slips in hand.

"Are you sure that's the way you want me to handle it?" I asked Dan and another assembler who had accompanied him to this meeting.

"Yes, everyone agrees that we want it all out in the open."

Figure **10.4** From Frozen Layer to Fear Defroster

I worried about the emotional trauma for the entire group, not just those who would lose their jobs. I had never had to do something this gut-wrenching, so I was also worried about my own emotional reaction. Since I did not want to break down in front them, I had figured one-on-one dismissals would make the task more tolerable.

I will never forget entering the room filled with nervous people, sitting down on a stool, and facing my team. I loved these hard-working and deeply committed people and could not bear the thought of saying goodbye to any of them. Over the next 30 minutes I slowly read the list of layoffs, one name at a time. Yes, we all shed a few tears, but the team also displayed great courage and compassion, applauding and hugging each person who would be leaving the team. It was one of the most horrible yet meaningful experiences of my management career. This shift is illustrated in Figure 10.4.

1. *Banish victim thinking.* When things go wrong, it's easy to feel sorry for yourself and blame someone else for the problem. Even if you become a victim of an unexpected setback, you can't move forward if you keep thinking like a victim. Move forward and people will follow. When you must dismiss Ellen from the team due to consistently poor performance, make sure no one, including yourself, succumbs to victim thinking. Her leaving represents an opportunity for you, the team, and Ellen to learn and grow.

2. *Remove fear words from your vocabulary.* Words carry powerful meanings for people, so it pays to do what a good

carpenter does: measure twice, cut once. Think before you speak. Many words frighten people. Compare "We had to fire Ellen for her lousy performance" to "We're helping Ellen find a position more suitable to her talents."

3. *Offer comfort and encouragement.* Just as people respond positively to admissions of vulnerability, they respect managers who display genuine caring, compassion, and empathy. They want to know you have their best interests at heart and share their pain. "I like Ellen and wish we could have kept her on the team. I spent a few hours with her talking about options that would suit her better, and she's looking forward to this next phase of her career."

From Commander to Inspirational Guide

Thirty days before the 2008 U.S. presidential election, Mark Cleveland, president and CEO of Swiftwick, a Brentwood, Tennessee, manufacturer of performance socks for athletes, received a phone call from a good friend presenting him with a challenge. Could Cleveland's company generate some national publicity by stitching "CHANGE" and a picture of candidate Barack Obama on a batch of its high-performance socks? Cleveland liked the idea but saw one huge obstacle: No other sock maker had ever pulled off such a feat in such a short period of time.

"It was impossible," Cleveland remembers saying when he first heard the idea. "No one had ever designed, produced, packaged, and shipped a sock in 48 hours. It takes 6 to 10 weeks to produce a new sock." Still, as an entrepreneur, he couldn't resist the challenge.

Rather than cracking a whip to make his people accomplish the impossible, Cleveland inspired his staff to set a new record. He understood that in such a situation people needed to work with their hearts as well as their heads. His rallying cry—"Why not do the impossible?"—won their hearts and inspired them to work feverishly to accomplish the mission. Sure enough, the first batch of Obama CHANGE socks shipped in less than 48 hours.

Thirty days later, Swiftwick had sold over a thousand pairs of Obama CHANGE socks, generating a lot of television coverage and

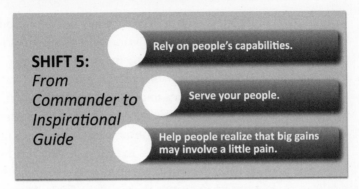

FIGURE **10.5** From Commander to Inspirational Guide

a front-page story, complete with full-color photo of the product on the front page of *The Oregonian*, Oregon's daily newspaper.

"We all learned we could be excellent in responding to an opportunity," explains Cleveland, reflecting back on the achievement. "It inspired us to go back and take a second run at the golf market, and today 20 percent of the pros on the Professional Golf Association tour are wearing our socks, not because we pay them to, because we can't afford that, but because our socks give them a competitive advantage." Swiftwick has been tripling sales every year since 2008.

Cleveland knew the capabilities of his employees, and interacted with them not as the CEO in control but as a coach and source of inspiration (see Figure 10.5). He acknowledged that the all-out effort might cause some suffering for them, but he also showed them that the potential gains could far outweigh the pain.

1. *Rely on people's capabilities.* Great leaders inspire people to apply their capabilities to fulfill their vision for the organization. They don't worry about why people might not get the job done; instead, they always ask "Why not?" When you ask your people that question, they will usually answer by enrolling in the effort. You can't order people to fly to the moon, but you can remind them they possess the power of science to do so.
2. *Serve your people.* Great leaders do not believe that people work for them, but that they work for their people. If you want

your staff to land safely on the moon, you can best help them get there by making it clear that you will work hard to give them all the resources they need to make the journey.

3. *Help people realize that big gains may involve a little pain.* As people apply their capabilities to accomplish the mission, they will make mistakes, suffer setbacks, and grow weary. Remind them that even the negative experiences along the way are learning experiences. Like athletes in training, their hard work will make them quicker and smarter and more effective. Nothing makes people happier than to feel their wings grow stronger as they keep moving toward the goal.

Creating New, Observable Behaviors

Renowned lawyer Alan Dershowitz recalled a breakfast he shared with Leona Helmsley at one of her famous New York City Helmsley Hotels. When the waiter brought Dershowitz a cup of tea that had a few drops of liquid splashed on the saucer, Helmsley, known by then as "The Queen of Mean," grabbed the cup from the waiter, smashed it on the floor, then demanded that the waiter get down on his knees and beg for his job. Her antics, though fascinating, were outrageous, and certainly not the kind of behavior any leader should ever emulate. Bad bosses make for good entertainment in the movies, from the sadistic chain-gang overseer who tortured Paul Newman's character in *Cool Hand Luke* to the imperious Gordon Gekko who terrorized colleagues and competitors alike in *Wall Street*.

If you work for one of these tyrants, your life can become a living hell, and not just as fallout from full-blown tantrums, but as well from the little slights and manipulations that can sting as much as a venomous public rebuke. Bad bosses care more about their own power than the welfare of their people; they try to control every move their employees make; they deliver swift and severe punishment for even minor mistakes. Past generations of workers may have silently suffered such treatment, but workers who bring the millennial mind-set to their work will not.

The best managers do not just think good thoughts, they do good deeds. They model the behavior they want their people to emulate. For your people to act in the now, you must demonstrate such actions

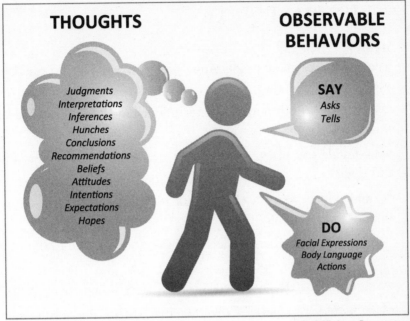

SOURCE: Jean Baumann

FIGURE **10.6** Observable Behaviors for the NOW workplace

yourself. People need to *see* you in action. It's more than leading the troops into battle; it's making your beliefs, your values, your ideals, your attitudes, your hopes and dreams, your fears, and your intentions observable to others. When you speak, people should most often hear a question mark at the ends of your sentences; and when you model a behavior, people should see it as something they can and should do themselves (see Figure 10.6).

Chapter 5 explored the NOW Mindset needed to shift the thinking and behavior of every single member of an organization's workforce. As a leader you must initiate, guide, and align these new thoughts and behaviors. By asking the right questions and doing the right things, you teach people a new way of thinking and acting, one that empowers them to work at the speed of now.

A good leader-teacher keeps asking questions that instill the five most important attributes of a NOW Mindset into a NOW organization. When you do that consistently, you drive home the most crucial lessons about doing *business at the speed of now.*

Lesson 1: I Use Facts to Find Truth

Ask:

"You make a great point, Ann. Can you get data to validate your theory?"

"What data would help us better understand the root cause of this problem?"

"Mike, can you create a chart that helps us better understand this data?"

"Could you develop a checklist of the data we need to better understand this issue?"

"That's interesting data, Nigel, but how does it relate to the root cause of this problem?"

"What additional data will shed light on what's causing this problem?"

"Tim, could you draw a diagram that shows the relationship between the cause and effect of this problem?"

Do:

Base your decisions on facts.

Master the data collection and presentation tools you want your people to use.

Become a superb data collector yourself.

Lesson 2: I Serve My Customers (Internal and External)

Ask:

"Can you name your customers, Julie?"

"David, can you describe your customers' needs?"

"Have you asked your customers about their needs?

"What does your customer think about your solution, Ralph?"

"If your customers could choose a service option, would they pick this one?"

"How do you measure your customer's level of satisfaction?"

"How would you describe your customer relationships?"

"Can you think of ways to address customer complaints more quickly and effectively?"

Do:
Get to know your own customers, especially your own people.

Design a system for gathering feedback from your customers.

Ask your customers to rate your performance.

LESSON 3: I IMPROVE MY PROCESSES

Ask:
"Richard, can you explain process mapping to me?"

"Could you walk me through your process, Adam?"

"Pat, can you show me where this process is breaking down?"

"Can you show me the map of your process, Billie?"

"How do you think we could streamline this process?"

"Do you see any opportunities to save time and costs with a process improvement effort?"

Do:
Learn how to map processes.

Map your own processes.

Teach others how to map their processes.

Look for ways to improve your processes.

Become an expert problem solver.

Lead a problem-solving project from start to finish.

LESSON 4: PEOPLE COUNT ON ME

Ask:
"John, do you understand how your work helps achieve the company's goals?"

"Can you describe how a breakdown in your process affects others?"

"LeAnn, do you thank your people for their contribution to your success?"

"Do you think people 'have your back' when the going gets tough?"

"Do you 'have their back' in tough situations?"

Do:

Remind yourself how your work helps achieve the company's goals.

Remain alert for breakdowns in your leadership that affect others.

Thank the people who contribute to your success.

Make sure your people know that you "have their backs."

LESSON 5: I KEEP SCORE TO MAINTAIN FOCUS

Ask:

"Bob, do you feel comfortable with the way we measure performance?"

"Can you share your latest process performance measures with me, Ellen?"

"Would you refine our measures to make them more accurate and useful?"

"Do the process measures help you keep focused on doing the work well?"

"How would you suggest I improve my own performance measures, Ralph?"

Do:

Establish accurate and useful performance measures.

Measure your own performance.

Ask for suggestions about improving your own measures.

Invite people to offer ideas about improving all performance measures.

Tell Me a Story

Steve Sabol, the creator of NFL Films, once said, "Tell me a fact, and I'll remember; tell me the truth, and I'll believe; but tell me a story, and I'll hold it in my heart forever." Great teachers inspire their students by asking the right questions and doing the right things, but they also know how to use the power of storytelling to drive home lessons in a memorable way.

The great teachers in history, from Plato, Aesop, Jesus, and Confucius to C. S. Lewis, Frank McCourt, and J. K. Rowling, enthralled their students with stories. The most influential and bestselling book of all time, the *Bible*, did not tell people how to live their lives, it *showed* them, using stories and parables. When people remember a good story, they remember its moral. In Aesop's fable "The Ant and the Grasshopper," the sensible ant prepares for the winter and thrives; the foolish grasshopper fritters away the summer and dies. Point taken, point remembered, for untold generations.

Collect good stories. Recall the events in your life and career that would make a good story to share with others. Learn how to tell a good story. Then tell it. This skill, along with asking questions and modeling behaviors, will make you a great teacher and a profound leader.

■ ■ ■

Complete the Speedometer for Becoming a NOW Leader in Table 10.1 and add your net score to the summary sheet in the Appendix.

TABLE 10.1   NOW Speedometer 10: Becoming a NOW Leader

Then	−1	0	+1	Now
We answer all questions with a yes or no				We answer questions with questions
We discourage people from taking initiative				We have leaders who constantly encourage taking initiative
We expect the boss to know all the answers				We expect people to look for their own answers
We do not expect a boss to apologize for making mistakes				We expect a boss to apologize for making mistakes
We make all changes from the top down				We make sure the vast majority of changes come from the bottom up
We do not see managers learning and growing every day				We see managers learning and growing every day
We do not expect managers to lead by example				We expect managers to lead by example
Subtotals				

Becoming a NOW Leader **NET SCORE**

Add this score to the consolidated score in the Appendix.

THEN		NOW
-7 -6 -5 -4 -3 -2 -1	0	+1 +2 +3 +4 +5 +6 +7

Embracing Change Now

Accelerate the Shift

Dr. John Snyder had a hunch. He strongly supported evidence-based oral healthcare at Permanente Dental Associates (PDA), one of the largest group dental practices in the United States. As a practicing general dentist, he had always treated patients with scientifically proven best practices. Shortly after he was elected CEO of the company, he contacted Mass Ingenuity about adopting our NOW Management System. Given the challenges he faced in the stressful world of healthcare, he thought our approach might be just what the doctor ordered.

Three years later his hunch proved right. "It just fit the same common-sense test that evidence-based care did. It uses data, identifies what does or doesn't work, and it drives toward prescribed, proven solutions. I have learned as a dentist that everything has a structure and a lot of repetition behind it. Management is no different."

Dr. Snyder had practiced dentistry for 23 years, but he had never run a business. PDA was a fairly big business, employing 125 dentists who contracted their services to Kaiser Foundation Health Plan, and with a support staff of 600 people in 17 clinics throughout Oregon and southwest Washington.

At the time he stood for election by his peers, he ran on a campaign of "uncompromised quality and unlimited potential." PDA had not, he believed, fulfilled that potential. The company faced many challenges.

"Our dentists were not really being given the opportunity to demonstrate their full capability. Once we figured out the business and the work we had to do, it was critical to make sure we lined people up with their passions and gave them the right structure and support."

As Dr. Snyder later recalled, "We had enjoyed some pockets of success because we have such a talented and committed group of dentists and staff. Then we took the time and did the work to really understand our business by building out our fundamentals. We took something that seemed so fragmented and created out of it tremendous clarity. Once we achieved that clarity, it simplified everything and made it easy to get focused."

A sharp focus on fundamentals and a series of impressive breakthroughs resulted in some impressive numbers, as you can see in Table 11.1.

Even in a climate of great economic uncertainty, between 2008 and 2010, PDA increased both its membership and enjoyed strong financial results.

TABLE 11.1 Permanente Dental Associates Results

Measure	2008	2010	Change	Definition
Dentist Engagement	71.2	77.3	+9%	Overall engagement rating on 100-point scale
Concern for Comfort	56.0	63.8	+14%	Percent patients rating "very good"
New Patient Access	6.2	3.1	−50%	Weeks to first appointment for new patients
General Dentist Access	4.4	3.5	−20%	Weeks to routine appointment for general dentist
Unfilled Dentist Hours	8.7	5.1	−41%	Percent of scheduled time with no patient to serve
Dentists Doing Oral Health Research	46.0	56.0	+22%	Percent dentists volunteering to do research
Dentist Turnover	5.9	3.2	−46%	Percent dentist annual turnover
Outcomes Measures on Plan	29.7	50.0	+68%	Percent of outcome targets achieved
Process Measures on Plan	50.0	73.1	+46%	Percent of process targets achieved

Data Courtesy of Permanente Dental Associates.

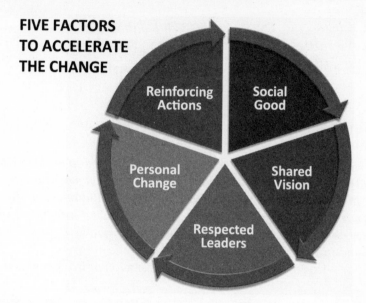

FIVE FACTORS TO ACCELERATE THE CHANGE

Reinforcing Actions

Social Good

Personal Change

Shared Vision

Respected Leaders

FIGURE 11.1   Five Change Factors

As PDA evolved into a true NOW organization, it became such an admired model in the industry that Dr. Snyder and the PDA dentists have been invited to tell their story at dental conferences around the world. The company had made a lot of changes in the way it does business, but its accomplishments rested on its emphasis on the same five crucial factors that drive any successful change effort: social good, shared vision, respected leaders, personal change, and reinforcing actions (see Figure 11.1). The shift started with a shared vision of PDA's role in delivering better healthcare, and it became a reality because PDA's respected leaders made personal changes and acted in ways that reinforced those changes.

Leaders can successfully transform any organization by:

1. Defining the *social good* in a way that inspires people to welcome change.
2. Promoting a *shared vision* of the future that inspires people to want to work toward the change.
3. Engaging *respected leaders* within the organization to teach and model desired behaviors.

4. Creating an agenda for *personal change*.
5. Promoting *reinforcing actions* that lead to successful transformation.

Working for the Social Good

"Our motto—Whole Foods, Whole People, Whole Planet—emphasizes that our vision reaches far beyond just being a food retailer. Our success in fulfilling our vision is measured by customer satisfaction, Team Member excellence and happiness, return on capital investment, improvement in the state of the environment, and local and larger community support."
  —Excerpt from Whole Foods' Declaration of Interdependence

Cynics argue that big corporations merely pay lip service to sustainability, ethics, and the greater social good, but companies like Whole Foods practice what they preach. They believe that corporate profitability and social responsibility can go hand in hand. In 1985, long before the notion of the social good came into vogue, the company's leaders asked 60 employees to create the company's Declaration of Interdependence. Updated three times since its creation, the declaration stresses such core values as "Creating wealth through profits and growth," and "Supporting team member excellence and happiness."

Its "social good" platform has attracted a special kind of employee, a special kind of supplier, a special kind of customer, and a special kind of success for the organization. In 2010, Whole Foods' year-over-year same-store sales grew 7.1 percent, compared to Safeway's 4.9 percent decline, Kroger Company's 0.9 percent growth, and SuperValu's 5.1 percent decrease. Whole Foods also significantly outperformed those same peers in revenue per square foot, gross margin, operating margin, and net profit margin. It turns out that social good *is* good business.

Dr. William Seidman, president and founder of Cerebyte, a consulting firm dedicated to helping clients harness change, believes that emphasis on the social good motivates people, provided they see it as a fair process. He explains: "In simple terms . . . during the change process, if people perceive they are being treated in a way that increases their dignity and personal sense of honor, their natural resistance is overcome and they embrace the change. Conversely, if people perceive that the change process somehow diminishes or marginalizes them, natural resistance becomes more intense, and they reject the change."

Whole Foods increases people's dignity and personal sense of honor by welding social good to its mission, vision, and values. Nike does the same thing when it ties social good to the company's belief in the value of individual motivation and physical fitness.

Microsoft offers another good example. "When Paul Allen and I started Microsoft over 30 years ago, we had big dreams about software," recalls Bill Gates in an article that appeared in *The Telegraph* when he relinquished his leadership role at the company some years ago. "We had dreams about the impact it could have. We talked about a computer on every desk and in every home. It's been amazing to see so much of that dream become a reality and touch so many lives. I never imagined what an incredible and important company would spring from those original ideas."

We at Mass Ingenuity believe so strongly in the power of working for the social good that we have built the concept into the NOW Management System. One client, Marti Lundy, retired CEO and cofounder of Moore Electronics, recalls, "The NOW Management System not only catapulted our company into the future with innovative new thinking and great results, it brought many employees great personal growth."

When an organization incorporates the social good into its mission, values, and routine work, it unleashes the talent, experience, creativity, energy, and passion of its people because it:

- Allows them to share their human gifts.
- Challenges them to learn and to grow.
- Provides them with the opportunity to make a difference.
- Connects them to others who share their values.
- Creates the opportunity for them to take true pride in their work.
- Affords them the respect of their peers.
- Enhances their self-esteem through meaningful accomplishment.

Sharing a Vision of the Future

Kris Kautz, deputy director of the Department of Administrative Services (DAS) for the State of Oregon knows the importance of building an organization's shared vision. "I did not imagine the impact this was going to have," she says. "We have never had a vision employees developed using their own words."

Both Kautz and then-director Scott Harra found their organization suffering from the effects of the 2008 recession. The steep decline of the economy and the painfully slow recovery added an incredible burden to an already challenging lack of confidence. DAS's employees, like many who work in government agencies, felt the effects of layoffs and a lack of trust for public employees. They came under constant fire from their customers, in this case people who worked at the other agencies served by DAS. To reverse that trend, our consulting firm began working with Harra and Kautz to install a more effective management system.

We helped the team develop a shared vision of what the agency would look like in five years. True to our philosophy, this shared vision would not come as an edict but from the people who would be doing the agency's daily work. "I was asked by the team that drafted it if the executive team was going to change the language," Kautz recalls. When she assured her people that no one would override the result, they took full ownership of the outcome. "They felt it was really their product."

One word best describes the shared vision created by the team: "hope." Hope was exactly what these people needed. It energized everyone, Kautz included. "It leaves me feeling just as hopeful as the people who wrote it. I, too, want to work for the organization it describes."

A shared vision needs to offer a lot of detail describing the future. In the case of the DAS vision statement, the entire document ran to nearly 1,000 words, so it's not possible to include it in its entirety here, but we can share a handful of key sentences that capture its spirit:

> *"People who work at the Department of Administrative Services know they make a significant difference for Oregon."*

"We provide leadership on behalf of the Governor to ensure accountability and wise use of state resources."

"Because we are a Lean operation that emphasizes streamlined processes, we are innovative and cost-effective."

"DAS engages with other state agencies to share professional knowledge and find common solutions to statewide problems. We are a leader in the nation."

"We understand and respond to our customers' needs. They value our outstanding service and responsiveness."

"The confidence and trust of our customers and stakeholders are very high."

"Our technological advances allow us to move faster, access information more quickly, and reduce paperwork."

"We pull our own weight, understanding we are ultimately accountable to the citizens of Oregon."

"We are innovative, flexible, and open to change."

"We are now in the forefront of new ideas, methods, and technology; being visionary, we focus on our future."

Most organizations develop some sort of vision statement, usually an inspiring phrase that describes an attribute the business wants to project to the world, or a major goal it wants to achieve. We, however, feel the ideal statement paints a vivid, detailed picture of the organization's future for all of its stakeholders. And the best ones come from the employees, not the leadership. A people-generated statement adds force to an organizational change effort, because it:

◆ Demonstrates to employees that leadership wants them deeply involved in shaping the organization's future.
◆ Clarifies the organization's future in a way that helps employees determine whether or not they can align with it.
◆ Provides a context for testing new ways to do the "right thing."
◆ Inspires receptivity to the changes that will make the vision a reality.
◆ Instills dignity and pride and self-esteem.

To make sure the shared vision delivers those benefits, an organization should review and, if necessary, revise its shared vision periodically.

Creation of the initial shared vision may involve 10 to 20 people in a large organization. Those individuals should represent all major functions, processes, and levels of authority; and leaders should choose them based on their reputations for trustworthiness, honesty, fairness, reliability, and other personal qualities that have won them credibility among their peers. At the Oregon Department of Administrative Services, the agenda for the first shared vision team meeting included such probing questions as:

◆ Why do you work here?
◆ What will it look like to work here in five years?
◆ What will employees say about working here?
◆ What will our customers say about us?
◆ What will our suppliers say about us?
◆ What will our organization's culture look like in five years?
◆ What will our physical work environment look like?
◆ What kind of measurable results will we achieve?
◆ What new skills will we have learned?
◆ Why will we want to still be working here in five years?

DAS team members took sufficient time to first collectively edit and then privately answer each question in their own words. The team then melded all the answers, identified themes, and developed a first draft of the shared vision document using selected phrases framed by members of the team. They then edited and reedited the draft, producing the finalized version they eventually shared with everyone else in the organization. But before it went out, leadership reviewed the shared vision, not to change it but to understand what the team members were thinking. Eventually, DAS started collecting reactions and suggestions from people across the organization in anticipation of further refining the document in the next iteration. (Note: Though DAS chose not do so, an organization could make good use of internal social media to gather widespread and timely feedback.)

DAS presented the final shared vision in a variety of ways, including a narrated PowerPoint presentation accompanied by a set of slides whose images reinforced each key element. The presentation was made available to all employees to watch and use via the department's intranet. Deputy Director Kautz made sure that it appeared on agendas for many DAS meetings, such as new employee orientations, Quarterly Target Reviews, Seven-Step Problem Solving, and Breakthrough initiatives.

Engaging the Most Respected Change Leaders

Upon the death of legendary basketball coach John Wooden, Bill Walton, former NBA star and sports commentator, wrote a tribute to the man who had taught him the art and science of basketball at UCLA. "And teach he did," said Walton, "everything as a matter of fact, on a constant basis, from showing us how to put our shoes and socks on, to how to get dressed properly so that our equipment and tools would never interfere with our goals and dreams, to how to build a foundation based on human values and personal characteristics . . . so that when you aren't hot, when you are not in the zone, when the ball bounces the other way, you will still be able to achieve peak performance on command."

Wooden led UCLA to an astonishing 88 consecutive NCAA wins over four seasons. During his 27 years at UCLA, his teams scored 620 wins against 147 losses, and won 10 NCAA championships over a 12-year period.

"John Wooden represents the conquest of substance over hype, the triumph of achievement over erratic flailing, the conquest of discipline over gambling, and the triumph of executing an organized plan over hoping that you'll be lucky . . . ," Walton concluded.

Dr. Seidman calls leaders like Wooden "positive deviants," by which he means people who display uncommon but successful behaviors and strategies that enable them to find better solutions to problems than their peers, even though they possess no greater resources or deeper knowledge. These respected change leaders exist in every organization and help accelerate the shift to the now. When you identify and involve these individuals in a change effort, others will join them in the campaign.

Change leaders consistently outperform others at whatever they do because their mental models, the rules of thumb they apply to

WHAT CHANGE LEADERS CONTRIBUTE

CHARACTERISTIC 1	CHARACTERISTIC 2	CHARACTERISTIC 3	CHARACTERISTIC 4
See the shift in visionary, socially responsible, and exciting terms.	Create comprehensive mental maps of roles, responsibilities, task definition, and workflow.	Recognize what can go wrong and take steps to prevent it.	Help people quickly and effectively resolve specific concerns and questions.

FIGURE 11.2　Contributions of Change Leaders

situations, their mechanisms for early problem detection, the way they focus their attention, and their work habits differ from their colleagues in significant ways, explains Seidman (see Figure 11.2).

They see change in visionary, socially responsible, and exciting terms.

"I see what we are doing in PDA as a possible solution for the crisis we face today with the costs of health care," Dr. Snyder tells his board and leadership team during a planning retreat.

Dr. Snyder rose from the ranks to become CEO in part because he understands the link between healthcare organizations and healthcare costs, and he speaks boldly about how his company and its people can make a difference in the world.

They create comprehensive mental maps of roles and responsibilities, task definition, and workflow.

"I know this is a different way of thinking so I want to help you see it very clearly," explained the facilities administrator for the State of Oregon's Department of Administrative Services to a group of employees.

The administrator gave her people a practical way to connect the work they do (managing vehicles, buildings, equipment, etc.) to the agency's core process of "managing assets." Given the complexity of the 59 measures they used, she came up with the ingenious idea of using a fancy layer cake to illustrate how it all fit together.

They anticipate what can go wrong, and take steps to prevent it.

"I know the temptation to jump to solutions early on in the process will be overwhelming," Brad Ritter cautions his team at Matrix Semiconductor. "So while I'm going to write down some of your suspected causes of the problem we are working on now, I am going to ask all of you to set these ideas aside until we gather enough data to feel confident we have found the true root cause."

Brad knows that leaping to premature conclusions can sabotage the problem-solving effort, so he frequently reinforces this point as the team moves toward a solution.

They help people quickly and effectively resolve concerns and questions.

"Let's sit down now and talk through your concerns, Carl," says Marti Lundy of Moore Electronics to her head of production as soon as she encounters resistance to writing a Breakthrough Plan.

When Lundy discovered that Carl felt frustrated using the Breakthrough Planning tool, she not only dealt with his resistance, she immediately reinforced its value to all managers in the organization.

Respected change leaders strongly influence others because they activate what neuroscientists call "mirror neurons." Those same mirror neurons make you feel upbeat and positive in the presence of someone who gets genuinely excited about an undertaking.

Many managers surround themselves with like-minded people, and they often select future leaders who think and act as they do. However, when it comes to transforming an organization from *then* to *now*, you should consider surrounding yourself with people who think and act *different* from you, people who have demonstrated an ability to welcome and even promote change. That often means individuals with the millennial mind-set, who grasp such new ideas as accessing information with cloud computing and using social media to build strong communities. Their enthusiasm will prove contagious.

Look also for people who pay attention to details without losing sight of the big picture. Was John Wooden a great basketball coach simply because he possessed a better mind for basketball? No, he set amazing records because he keenly focused his mind on all the mundane, detailed, repetitive, and practical details of the game. His tremendous persistence and discipline and the results he achieved speak volumes about buckling down and doing the detailed work that's required to achieve a goal—any goal.

Encouraging Personal Change

Earlier in this chapter we introduced Marti Lundy, the retired former co-owner of Moore Electronics who not only talked about working for the social good but also experienced the power of encouraging personal change. "Once we made the commitment, there was no turning back," she said. Every one of her top managers had come to her at some point, expressing doubt about continuing with the shift to the NOW Management System. Lundy chose to stay the course. "Although we struggled at times, I did not allow us to deviate from the commitment we had made to implement the change."

Lundy maintained her commitment for both idealistic and practical reasons, despite the loss of some people who could not accept the need for change. To her mind, the company's traditional command-and-control approach to managing the business was not fully tapping the company's richest resource, its people. Unless Moore Electronics released that potential, she did not think the company could profitably meet the increasingly demanding needs of such customers as Medtronic, Hewlett-Packard, Agilent Technologies, and Novellus. Customer needs were driving up costs, and Moore's people were not finding ways to deliver higher quality and still make a profit. Lundy decided that only a radical new approach could save the day.

"Early in my career I worked for Hewlett-Packard and was exposed to some very impressive business practices," recalls Lundy. While she and her partner fully agreed on the goals for their company, they held divergent perspectives on how best to reach those goals. To avoid a major clash, the two decided that each of them would run the company for three years and that Lundy would take the first shift. Could she prove that her approach would work in that short time?

At the outset Lundy set her sights on three issues:

Issue number one: Moore went through phases of feast or famine. "When the business was growing, we went into chaos, and then when it slacked off, we starting laying people off," she explains. The up-and-down syndrome had become predictable, and reacting to it the same way each time did not make sense to her.

Issue number two: Moore's current organization of departments into compartmentalized silos prevented staff from applying their full array of talents and skills.

Issue number three: Moore's top managers, schooled in a traditional command-and-control approach, resisted making any major changes. "When I talked to my team about the changes I felt we needed to make, they were all enthusiastic. But once we got into it, and they discovered they had to learn to do things differently, the change became a lot more personal. We started getting at their egos. 'I am good at what I do or I wouldn't be in this role . . . so why do I need to change and do things differently?'"

Lundy adopted the NOW Management System to address all three issues simultaneously, and over the three ensuing years her intuition proved correct as Moore enjoyed its highest level of performance ever. That performance hinged on people making personal changes throughout the company.

To help Lundy get her people aboard the change effort, we suggested she study the classic hero's journey that Joseph Campbell describes in his book, *The Hero with a Thousand Faces*, illustrated in Figure 11.3.

Campbell argues that throughout history and across all cultures the human race's great success stories involve the same seven-step pattern:

Step 1: Call to Action. The journey begins with excitement and anticipation. Middle manager Katherine enthusiastically embarks on the path to change because she thinks the new approach to

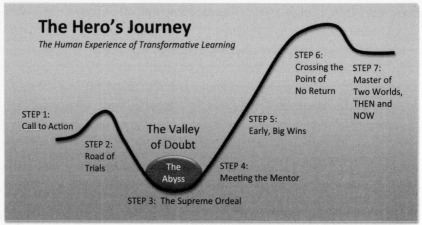

Adapted from Joseph Campbell's insights in *The Hero with a Thousand Faces*

FIGURE 11.3   Campbell's Hero's Journey

management will create greater success for herself, her team, and the company.

Step 2: Road of Trials. The hero continues the journey but encounters obstacles and setbacks along the way. As Katherine moves forward with the change effort and runs into detours and roadblocks, she worries about her ability to make the required changes.

Step 3: The Supreme Ordeal. The hero never abandons the journey even when painful events make it hard to continue. When Katherine's people threaten to quit because they do not see the value of all the sweeping changes in the company, she decides to return the phone call from the headhunter who told her about a job where she can return to the comfortable management approach that never caused this much pain.

Step 4: Meeting the Mentor. The journey proceeds to the Valley of Doubt, where the hero meets someone who offers understanding, support, and encouraging advice. At dinner with the retired executive who recruited her for her first management position, Katherine expresses her self-doubt and feels enormous relief when the woman confides her own experience with the same sort of feelings.

Step 5: Early, Big Wins. The journey's initial results reinforce its importance and energize the hero to press forward. Katherine's problem-solving team uncovers the root cause of a problem that has plagued the company for three years, and that major accomplishment inspires everyone to look for other opportunities for additional improvements in processes and performance.

Step 6: Crossing the Point of No Return. The hero can now see the journey's end, and mounting successes make it possible to begin enjoying the ultimate reward. When the headhunter calls Katherine again, she tells him she loves her current company and sees an unlimited future there.

Step 7: Master of Two Worlds. The journey's end prompts reflection, with the hero enjoying the benefits of understanding both the old and new order. Meeting again with her mentor, Katherine tells her that she feels that she has grown immeasurably by making major changes in the way she manages, and that her memory of the old ways will keep her on course to an even better direction.

Every transition entails a hero's journey. During your career you have made and will make similar journeys; understanding Campbell's model helps you view your past journeys and negotiate future ones.

As Lundy discovered, understanding made the journey much easier. "Every one of my top managers have gone on, and are having incredibly successful careers," she says now, some years after selling her company and moving on to new journeys.

Reinforcing the Right Actions

Dr. Seidman has studied what neuroscience can teach businesspeople about management training and its impact on people's attitudes and thought and behavior patterns. Results from magnetic resonance imaging (MRI) technology has helped researchers to replace with hard science a lot of what social scientists have for a long time believed about the psychology of work and organizational development. Thanks to MRI technology, scientists can actually see, in real time, how the human brain responds to various stimuli.

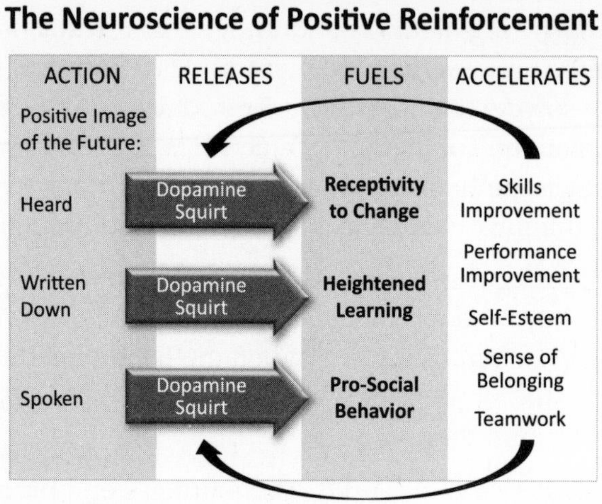

The Neuroscience of Positive Reinforcement

ACTION	RELEASES	FUELS	ACCELERATES
Positive Image of the Future:			
Heard	Dopamine Squirt	Receptivity to Change	Skills Improvement
			Performance Improvement
Written Down	Dopamine Squirt	Heightened Learning	Self-Esteem
			Sense of Belonging
Spoken	Dopamine Squirt	Pro-Social Behavior	Teamwork

FIGURE 11.4 Cycle of Positive Reinforcement

"When we see things in very positive terms, there is a release of neurotransmitters that create a feeling of well-being," explains Seidman. "This release is known as a dopamine 'squirt.' Dopamine itself is associated with positive interests in things, and research shows that in the state of being positive, people's openness to new ideas, and their ability to learn, spike."

Inputs from activities such as hearing, writing, drawing, and talking stimulate different parts of the brain (see Figure 11.4). If someone in a work environment reads a shared vision out loud, the spoken words trigger a release of dopamine in the brains of those who hear it. The same occurs when listeners write down the points in the shared vision that impressed them the most, and again when they tell others about their impressions. These chemical reactions increase receptivity to change, speed up learning, augment capability, and heighten positive social behavior. Skill improvement contributes to performance improvement; performance improvement results in a greater sense of self-esteem; and improved self-esteem increases people's sense of belonging, which enhances teamwork. Dopamine triggers include the words and actions of the effective leader presented in Chapter 10, from questions that stimulate creative thinking to sincere expressions of gratitude for a job well done. Questions that prompt a search for solutions, and praise that rewards a successful search, reinforce success and create receptivity for more change.

Dr. John Snyder, Marti Lundy, Kris Kautz, and John Wooden understood that cycle, as have all the great leaders throughout history who have taken the hero's journey and changed their worlds.

The End of the Beginning

This marks the end of this book's journey, but it also marks the beginning of a brighter future for your organization. The journey from managing in the then to managing in the now does not differ from the hero's journey, and it always includes predictable experiences and struggles. It's no coincidence that the hero's seven steps on the path to success parallels the 11 chapters of this book when viewed as 11 steps.

I chose to end the book with this chapter because it pulls together a lot of what I have been saying all along about the transition from then to now. *It's all about change.* The more skillfully you learn to manage change and help your people embrace and make the right changes, the better your chances of firing them up to thrill your customers and crush your competition.

. . .

Complete the Speedometer for Embracing Change Now in Table 11.2 and add your net score to the summary sheet in the Appendix.

TABLE **11.2**　NOW Speedometer 11: Embracing Change Now

Then	–1	0	+1	Now
We do not connect what we do to the social good				We connect what we do to the social good
We do not encourage people to talk openly about their ideas and passions				We encourage people to talk openly about their ideas and passions
We have not created a detailed shared vision				We have created a detailed shared vision
We do not constantly communicate the shared vision				We constantly communicate the shared vision
We expect senior leadership to create our vision				We had a team of employees create our shared vision
We do not identify and encourage change leaders in our workforce				We identify and encourage change leaders in our workforce
We have not adopted a rigorous change program				We have adopted a rigorous change program
Subtotals				
Embracing Change Now **NET SCORE**				

Add this score to the consolidated score in the Appendix.

SPEEDOMETER

THEN		NOW
-7 -6 -5 -4 -3 -2 -1	0	+1 +2 +3 +4 +5 +6 +7

Conclusion
Do It Now!

"We have been going out of business for 40 years," quipped Alan Mulally, CEO of the Ford Motor Company, the very same company that had launched the era of mass production over 100 years ago. He spoke those words to his employees in a February 2007 speech, just five months after he had been chosen to take the helm of the troubled auto manufacturer and guide its turnaround.

That was *then*. This is *now*.

Mulally led a management revolution at Ford, boldly rescuing the company from a slow, painful demise. He borrowed $23.6 billion by mortgaging all of Ford's assets, sold off its side brands (Jaguar, Aston Martin, Volvo, Land Rover, and its stake in Mazda), negotiated huge compensation cuts with the unions (hourly costs dropped from $76 to $55 per hour), and unloaded all but one of the company's corporate jets. He also reinvigorated the stalled Taurus brand, pushed hard on developing hybrids, shifted the marketing focus to social media, and installed his famous 8:00 AM Thursday morning Business Plan Review.

On the *Harvard Business Review* blog, Tony Schwartz observed, "The day I was there, one Ford executive described a significant shortfall on a key projection. No one cringed, including Mulally, and the executive calmly outlined his suggested solutions. Then he invited others to share their ideas."

The shift from managing in the *then* to managing in the *now* quickly paid off. In 2010, two measures of productivity at Ford, sales and net income per employee, soundly beat General Motors and Daimler. Ford pulled in $786,000 in sales per employee and $40,000 in net income per employee, compared to GM's $671,000 and $25,000 and Daimler's $542,000 and $26,000. As a result of these accomplishments, *CNN Money* reported that Mulally became the eighth-highest-paid U.S. CEO in 2010, earning $26.5 million in cash and stock compensation.

Mulally also pulled one of the biggest dinosaurs of the mass production era out of its grave and set it on the road to *business at the speed of now*. Your challenges may never match the enormity of those Alan Mulally confronted, but they will equally test your management expertise in the months and years ahead.

The methodology for change remains the same, whether for a giant corporation, an operating unit, a department or function, a team, a process, or even one person's daily work. It begins with writing a capability Breakthrough Plan (see Chapter 6 for details). Your own unique Breakthrough Plan will set you on the road to doing *business at the speed of now*. Use the template provided here, along with the helpful guidelines following, for completing your plan. Fill in the blanks to capture your organization's specific challenges. Add space as needed. Writing these plans takes a little practice to make them robust and powerful. If you would like feedback on your plan, please use the online version, which you will find at http://NOW-Breakthrough-Plan. One of our team members will gladly provide you with input on your plan.

Then-to-Now Breakthrough Plan

Organization Name: _____

Objective:

_____
_____
_____
_____
_____

TARGETS:

_____
_____
_____
_____
_____

SITUATION:

_____

_____

_____

_____

_____

STRATEGIES:

_____

_____

_____

_____

_____

Guidelines for an Effective Plan

Objective: Write a concise one-sentence description of the result you want to achieve. Make it qualitative, rather than quantitative. For example: "To increase the frequency of saying yes to opportunities."

Targets: Compose a list of concrete, time-specific, and measurable results that will tell you that you have achieved your objective. For example, "Implement 20 ideas per employee by January 1, 2013."

Situation: Write as many sentences as it takes to capture a quantitative and qualitative description of the current situation, compared to the objective and overall targets, including obstacles to overcome and opportunities to seize. For example: "1. We scored –34 on our NOW Speedometer but have no plan to reach +34 or better."

Strategies: Strategies include a number of mini-objectives, whose achievement will result in reaching the overall objective. Each strategy responds to a specific element of the situation. Write these sentences as desired outcomes. For example: "1. All of our managers know immediate steps they must take to raise our NOW Speedometer score to +34 or better."

We advise you to periodically revise and update your plan, to reflect changes in personnel, customer demands, and competitive pressure. Use this ever-evolving outline to help you keep your eye on the ball—to keep your people highly motivated, surpass your customer's expectations, and stay well ahead of your most aggressive competitors.

We invite you to join the *Business at the Speed of Now* community at http://business-at-the-speed-of-now.com. There you can join an ongoing discussion of new ways to prepare for and succeed in a future that is sure to present even greater challenges than those we all face today.

Appendix

The NOW Speedometer:
Doing Business at the Speed of Now

After you complete each chapter, record your NOW Speedometer score in Table A.1. Your total score reflects the degree to which your organization currently functions at the speed of now. In the right-hand box, note any major opportunities you think your organization might seize in order to improve your score. Of course, you will want to concentrate most on those elements where you recorded your lowest scores.

TABLE A.1 Summary Speedometer

		NET SCORE	NOTE MAJOR KEY OPPORTUNITIES
1	CHAPTER 1 Working in the Now		
2	CHAPTER 2 Making the Shift to Now		
3	CHAPTER 3 Seizing the NOW Opportunity		
4	CHAPTER 4 Leveraging the NOW Game Changers		
5	CHAPTER 5 Working IN the NOW Business		
6	CHAPTER 6 Working ON the NOW Business		
7	CHAPTER 7 Creating NOW Transparency		
8	CHAPTER 8 Solving Problems Now		
9	CHAPTER 9 Enabling the NOW Workforce		
10	CHAPTER 10 Becoming a NOW Leader		
11	CHAPTER 11 Enabling Change Now		
	YOUR ORGANIZATION'S NOW SCORE		

Here's how to interpret your results:

TABLE A.2 NOW Summary Speedometer

Your Speed	What It Means
–77 to –56	Your organization is functioning completely in the *then* world, dangerously inflexible and unresponsive. It fails to capitalize on its people's talent and capabilities. Do everything you can to make it more flexible and responsive. Otherwise, your competitors will probably put you out of business.
–55 to –34	Your organization is functioning mostly in the *then* world. In order to tap your employees' full talents and capabilities, and compete more effectively in the marketplace, you need to implement some major changes that will get your people seizing opportunities and solving problems now.
–33 to –11	Your organization has begun to edge out of the *then* world, but it must make many more of the vital changes that will get it functioning fully in the now.
–10 to +10	Your organization has made some significant progress toward getting out of the *then* world and fully into the *now* world, but you must do a lot more work to accomplish the transformation.
+11 to +33	Your organization has moved about halfway into the *now* world. It displays a certain amount of agility and has begun tapping its people's talent for seizing opportunities and solving problems. You must not sit back and relax, however; it's essential to press firmly forward before you can reap the full rewards of functioning in the now.
+34 to +55	Your organization has become highly adaptive, with people routinely seizing opportunities and solving problems in the now. But you must continue to refine and improve its ability to operate at the speed of now.
+56 to +77	Congratulations! Your organization has fully accomplished the transition from *then* to *now*. You must remain vigilant, however, because major and unanticipated crises may strike at any time.

About the Author

John M. Bernard has been inspiring leaders to rethink how they run their organizations for 30 years. An experienced executive, consultant, and founder and chairman of Mass Ingenuity, John ardently challenges conventional management philosophy. Over the past 25 years, he has been fine-tuning a system of management that eliminates the gap between what leaders envision and employees deliver, enabling a vision that every opportunity can be effectively pursued by every employee every time.

He has sat in nearly every seat around the leadership table, from founder/CEO of a start-up firm to senior vice president of a multibillion-dollar financial services company with responsibilities for a workforce of a thousand. At Omark Industries, Electro Scientific Industries, Floating Point Systems, and StanCorp Financial Group his responsibilities ranged from communications, strategic planning, operations, information technology, marketing, and quality assurance to transforming a manufacturing plant that produced midrange-class supercomputers. His consulting work has spanned the globe in high-tech, service, distribution, utilities, banking, insurance, manufacturing, healthcare, education, and government. Nike, Baxter Healthcare, Kaiser Permanente, Tektronix, PacifiCorp, and Standard Insurance, and more than one hundred other companies around the world, have benefited from his expertise.

John resides in Oregon with his wife, Lannah, and their five-year-old twin daughter and son. He has also raised three grown daughters and has two grandchildren.

Index